OUTCAST LONDON
A Christian Response

OUTCAST LONDON
A Christian Response

The West London Mission
of the Methodist Church
1887–1987

Philip S. Bagwell

EPWORTH PRESS

British Library Cataloguing in Publication Data

Bagwell, Philip S.
Outcast London: a Christian response: the
West London Mission of the Methodist
church 1887–1987.
1. West London Mission——History
I. Title
266'.75421   BV2865

ISBN 0–7162–0435–5

First published 1987
by Epworth Press
Room 190, 1 Central Buildings
Westminster, London SW1H 9NR

Typeset at The Spartan Press Ltd,
Lymington, Hants
and printed in Great Britain by
Oxford University Press

Contents

List of Illustrations

between pages 98 and 99

We are grateful to the *Methodist Recorder* for permission to reproduce plate 1 (John Newton) and plate 15, and to the BBC Hulton Picture Library for plate 2.

LINE DRAWINGS
by Alan Brooks

Foreword by Lord Soper

History, as the immortal authors of *1066 and All That* have reminded the unwary, is not the record of what has happened (there is so much of it that as yet remains unrecorded); it is what people remember, and furthermore such memory is invariably selective. What follows this Foreword makes no attempt to deny this aphorism. This history of the West London Mission is culled from the memories of them who have worked in it, thought about it, and prayed for it. As one of that number I commend it to the reader, and I have no hesitation in asserting that it is very much worth reading as a documentation of a worthwhile endeavour in the name of Christian belief and obligation.

At the same time the significance of this story is reinforced when it is set against the background of events and conditions which in retrospect link these reminiscences with much more permanent conditions and movements. Many were not fully appreciated as they happened, but need to be considered if that deeper significance is to be recognized. It is because I am convinced of this wider relationship in the day-by-day, and year-by-year work of the West London Mission that I invite the prospective reader to put the story as it unfolds into this wider frame.

Here, then, is something of that background. To begin with it is no accident that the West London Mission's beginnings coincided with the impact upon Victorian England of *The Bitter Cry of Outcast London*. I recommend to the reader the importance of the relationship of the Methodist Forward Movement to the beginnings of the Mission. It served to highlight a church response to the implications of that 'bitter cry' – a response of which Methodism may well be proud – and the lack of it elsewhere among other churches, which should cause much organized Christianity to be ashamed.

Such a comment leads inexorably to a second theological frame

ix

in which to set the Mission's work. From its earliest days and through all its vicissitudes the Mission demonstrated the truth that personal salvation and social redemption were the obverse and the reverse of the same medal. Throughout its history the vision of the Kingdom of God was dominant and in some respects unique. The church at its best today is the residuary legatee of this unbreakable unity in the gospel between individual piety and corporate morality. The intensity and range of the Mission's commitments in answer to the 'bitter cry' of those who are life's outcasts is worthy to rank with the best churchmanship of this century.

I have space to indicate two other basic principles to which the West London Mission offers evidence. Enlightened civil government, more often than not, inherits rather than precedes the work of voluntary organizations. The West London Mission has been the bell-wether of social care which has been undertaken as an adventure in collective responsibility, and which has in turn been followed by the state. Crèches for children and work among alcoholics are among the examples of this truth.

The other is the flexibility of any enterprise which seeks to answer the questions which are being asked, and meet real needs as they arise or develop in an ever-changing situation. I invite the reader to see in the pages of this saga how adaptable has been the response of the West London Mission to the actual world in which its ministry has been set. In no spirit of complacency it claims to represent a gospel which is not fossilized in the past but supremely alive to the present, and ready to meet the future with the same spirit which has characterized its continuing ministry.

Donald Soper

Introduction

The West London Mission, established a century ago, was much more than just another Christian church. Within the Methodist Church it was the spearhead of the 'Forward Movement' whose leaders shared with John Ruskin the view that 'if our religion is good for anything it is good for everything'. They considered that the mainstream of Victorian Methodism had concentrated too exclusively – and selfishly – on the salvation of the individual soul. The founder of the Mission, Hugh Price Hughes, wrote in the *First Annual Report* in 1888 that 'the ethical teaching of Christ is applicable to business, pleasure and politics, as well as prayer meetings and sacraments'. It is for this reason that an attempt has been made here to place the history of the Mission in the context of the changing economic and social life of the people of London. It is hoped that by so doing the changes in the pattern of social work activities of the Mission may be better understood.

The preparation of this book has been a collective undertaking and I acknowledge, with gratitude, the help given by many people. Lord Soper answered numerous questions and recalled events covering half the life-span of the Mission. The Revds John Newton and Ken Howcroft read and commented on large parts of the typescript. John Hicks, whose knowledge of the Hinde Street Church is unrivalled, gave unstintingly of his time and resources. The Revds Arthur Shaw and Arnold Cooper both gave detailed reports of the life and activities of the Hinde Street Church in the post-war era. The very useful flow chart of the activities and locations of the West London Mission was compiled by Alan Brooks, who was also responsible for assembling the photographic and other illustrations. I wish to thank Angela Bibb, Nora Fuidge, Gwyneth Heady and Marianne Sekules who spared the time to conduct research in the records of the Hinde Street Church and the West London Mission, at Westminster City Archives and the Greater London Record Office.

The following friends wrote to me, lent me books and papers, or helped in other ways which proved invaluable in piecing together the record of events and activities: The Revd Derek Bibb, Wendy Delamore, Gertrude Evans, Alison Gowman, Jane Hutton, Kath Humphreys, Ethel Kent, Gordon Slater, Molly Turner, Yvonne Walker, Bill Weston and Winnie Wintringham. Special thanks are due to Brenda Bridges who transformed a grubby and much amended manuscript into an immaculate typescript. I accept sole responsibility for any errors that appear in the book.

In the preparation of this work I have been given every encouragement by my wife, Rosemary, who has put up with a larger than usual accumulation of books and papers and a less than usual level of help with the domestic chores. Her name could well be put alongside mine on the title page!

1 September 1986   Philip S. Bagwell

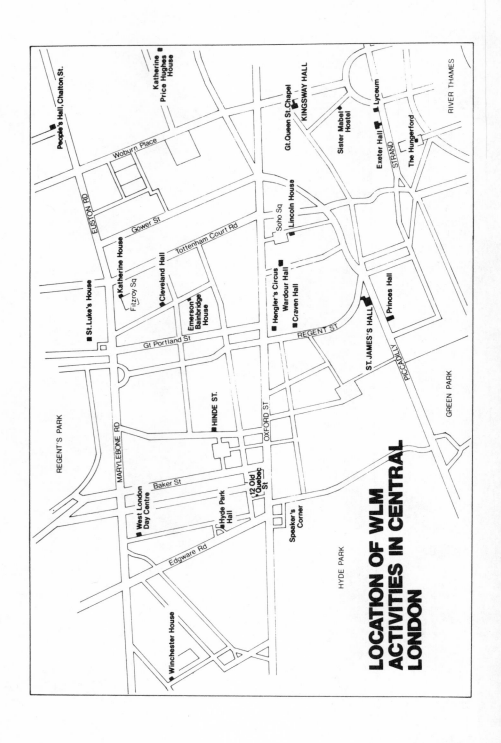

LOCATION OF WLM
ACTIVITIES IN CENTRAL
LONDON

1

London in the 1880s

In sharp contrast with the 1980s when the Greater London region had the *lowest* level of unemployment in the country (although containing important areas of severe deprivation), London in the 1880s had a greater proportion of its work-force jobless than did any other part of Britain. Agricultural workers from East Anglia, made redundant by the introduction of new harvesting machinery and the importation of cheap American wheat; dockers out of work because of the depression in trade, and many others, swelled the numbers of the unemployed in the worst years to as high as thirteen per cent of the work-force.[1] The influx of hundreds of thousands of persons into the metropolis greatly aggravated the housing shortage. Rents rocketed. Professor Alfred Marshall, the leading economist of the day, wrote that:

> The employer pays his high rent out of his saving in wages; and they have to pay their high rents out of their diminished wages. This is the fundamental evil.[2]

Friedrich Engels warned of the possible consequences at the time:

> Each succeeding winter brings up afresh the great question 'What to do with the unemployed?' But while the number of unemployed keeps swelling from year to year there is nobody to answer the question; and we can almost calculate the moment when the unemployed, losing patience, will take their fate into their own hands.[3]

Some twenty thousand of the unemployed did lose patience, in the midst of an exceptionally severe winter, on 8 February 1886, when they stormed out of Trafalgar Square and, provoked by jeers from members of the Carlton Club, smashed hundreds of windows and dozens of shops in the Mall. Within two days the Lord Mayor's fund for the relief of distress in the capital shot up from £19,000 to £72,000.[4] At that time there was no unemployment insurance: the alternatives were a precarious dependence on spasmodic charity or a resort to the workhouse.

The Revd Andrew Mearns, Secretary of the London Congregational Union, had an intimate knowledge of the life of Inner London and was deeply concerned with the human consequences of unemployment and poverty. In so far as any one event contributed to the founding of the West London Mission it was the publication, in October 1883, of his twenty-page penny pamphlet with the arresting title of *The Bitter Cry of Outcast London*. This unpretentious-looking publication has been described by a leading historian as 'perhaps the most influential single piece of writing about the poor that England has ever seen'.[5]

In his pamphlet, Mearns warned that:

> Whilst we have been building our churches and solacing ourselves with our religion and dreaming that the millennium was coming, the poor have been growing poorer, the wretched more miserable and the immoral more corrupt; the gulf has been daily widening which separates the lowest classes of the community from our churches and chapels, and from all decency and civilization.

Within a short walk of the wealthy clubs of Pall Mall and the millionaire mansions of Park Lane were 'pestilential human rookeries' where tens of thousands were 'crowded together amidst horrors which called to mind the middle passage of a slave ship'. Mearns and his Christian missioner assistants found hundreds of instances where whole families were living in one room, frequently but eight feet square:

> In one cellar a sanitary inspector reports finding a father, mother, three children and four pigs. In another room a missionary found a man ill with smallpox, his wife just recovering from her eighth confinement, and the children running about half naked and covered with dirt. Here are seven people living in one underground kitchen, and a little dead child lying in the same room . . . Here is a mother who turns her children into the street in the early evening because she lets her room for immoral purposes until long after midnight when the poor little wretches creep back again.

Immorality, it was maintained, was 'but the natural outcome of conditions like these'.

Christian men and women were particularly shocked by Mearns's statement that, 'Incest is common; and no form of vice or sensuality causes surprise or attracts attention.' They were appalled to learn that 'in one street of thirty-five houses thirty-two were brothels'. Attendance at church was a rarity. One street off Leicester Square contained 246 families, 'only twelve of which were represented in "the House of God"'.

Mearns blamed the slum landlords, who charged excessive rents – often 5s. 6d. for one small room when the family income might be less than £1 per week – for property that was fit only for demolition. 'The State must make short work of this iniquitous traffic,' he declared, 'and secure for the poorest the rights of citizenship; the right to live in something better than fever dens; the right to live as something better than the uncleanest of beasts. This must be done before the Christian missionary can have much chance with them.'

In addition to demanding new housing legislation, he advocated 'the erection of a mission hall in each district having appliances and conveniences requisite for the successful prosecution of the mission'.[6]

That Mearns's pamphlet attracted so much attention was largely due to the publicity given to it by the famous editor, W. T. Stead, who printed long extracts from it in his London daily newspaper *The Pall Mall Gazette* on 16 October 1883, and, in the same issue, supported Mearns's demand for urgent legislative action.

> These fever dens are said to be the best paying property in London and owners who, if justice were done, would be on the treadmill, are drawing from fifty to sixty per cent on investments in tenement property in slums.

In a further editorial a week later he returned to the attack:

> The man who lives by letting a pestilential dwelling house is morally on a par with a man who lives by keeping a brothel and ought to be branded accordingly.

Stead was 'inundated with letters from all parts of the kingdom' and on 22 October he wrote that, 'On no question that has been raised for many years does public interest appear to be so keen and deep.' Although one correspondent ('Plain Truth') blamed the crisis on 'insensate and reckless multiplication of the human species', most of those who wrote to Stead – and their number included many clergymen – conceded that social action as well as individual reformation or conversion was desperately needed.

– II –

Mearns's influence on the Christian churches, and especially on Wesleyan Methodism, was pervasive. His insistence that living conditions had to be improved 'before the Christian missionary can have much chance' marked 'a re-focusing of reform energies away from personal reformation to environmentalism'. Many Methodist ministers did not accept this change of emphasis. The Revd Foster Crozier, Superintendent of the Southwark circuit, while accepting that the facts as set out in *The Bitter Cry* were correct, stressed that there were Christian homes even in the slums. He advocated the provision of more chapels on the basis of one chapel seat to every ten of the population. He claimed that 'insufficiency of religious accommodation [was] not remotely, but intimately connected with, and *largely the cause of*, the depraved characters of many of the people' (my italics).[7]

He was supported in these views by the Revd Surman Cooke, who told his Bromley (Kent) Wesleyan congregation that the

> conditions described in *Bitter Cry* were explained mainly by the sin of these classes . . . no better housing, no sanitation, pressing as were these questions, would solve the question of 'outcast London' without salvation. Unless there were a great religious revival the outlook would be dark for the nation. London was the greatest mission field in the world.

Whatever the differences of view about the remedy for the evil, there is no doubt that the churches were stung into action by Mearns's exposure of the physical deprivation and spiritual destitution of the people living in the inner city. Innumerable sermons were preached, conferences were held and renewed mission activity and charitable organization took place.[8]

2

The Forward Movement:
Ferment within Methodism

– I –

One of those greatly influenced by *The Bitter Cry* was the Revd
Hugh Price Hughes, a young and very energetic Wesleyan minister
who took up the superintendency of the important Brixton Hill
circuit in South London soon after the pamphlet was published.
Hugh Price Hughes was born at Carmarthen on 8 February 1847,
the son of John Hughes, a surgeon, and Ann Phillips, the grand-
daughter of a Jewish banker in Haverfordwest. At first his parents
expected him to take up a legal career, but, influenced by the
fact that his grandfather was a Methodist minister, he opted
instead to follow that example. In a brief letter to his father he
wrote:

> My dear Father,
> I think I ought to be a Wesleyan Minister.
> Your affectionate son.

To which he received an equally brief reply:

> My dear Boy,
> I would rather that you should be a Wesleyan Minister than Lord
> Chancellor.
> Your affectionate Father.[1]

He was trained at the Wesleyan Theological College, Richmond,
Surrey, and later graduated both BA and MA at the University of
London.

While acting as a Bible Class teacher at Richmond in 1868 he fell
in love with Katherine, the fifteen-year-old daughter of the Principal, Alfred Barrett. Both sets of parents were agreed that

Katherine was too young to be engaged and that the couple should cease all communication with each other for three years. If they were then still of like mind the matter would be reconsidered. At that time Hughes 'was a decided Conservative and held aristocratic views as to the proper condition of the working classes'. He had a 'mild scorn for temperance', while his views on the position of women 'were quite the orthodox views of the day'.[2]

When they met again three years later, their determination to marry undiminished, Katherine found a man 'taking to heart the social inequalities and miseries of the working class . . . and an ardent supporter of the temperance movement'. In that interim he had been sent to minister in the Dover circuit and had been greatly influenced there by Alderman Rees, another passionate Welsh Methodist, to adopt a liberal and humanitarian creed. He had also been taken to hear Josephine Butler, the noted suffragist and campaigner against the Contagious Diseases Acts (1864, 1866, 1869), whose views left a deep impression on him and made him more sympathetic towards Katherine's feminist outlook.[3] These experiences no doubt helped to consolidate their married life, which began at Brighton on 20 August 1873. On leaving Brighton in September 1875 the Hughes's gained further experience of city life in Tottenham (1875–8), Dulwich (1878–81) and Oxford (1881–4) before moving to Brixton.

– II –

It was at one of the evening meetings held in the Raleigh Hall of the Brixton Hill circuit that the term 'Forward Movement' originated. In the course of an animated discussion on whether or not Methodists should concern themselves with social problems, Mrs Alexander McArthur said: 'We all belong to the Forward Movement here.' From that day the name stuck.[4] Dr Inglis's uncomplimentary comment was that: 'It was a vague concept made no less vague by Hughes's own attempt to clarify it.'[5] Nevertheless, its adherents had a shrewd notion of what it implied. Hughes had been 'stirred to the depths of his being' by the revelations in *The Bitter Cry*,[6] and was more than ever convinced that Methodism had been 'selfishly individualistic' in concentrating solely on personal salvation. The older view was that 'you cannot make people moral by Act of Parliament'. Hughes countered this by asserting that the law could certainly make them immoral, and cited the legislation on the liquor traffic to sustain his point. Law was 'educational as well as coercive', since people sometimes learned better·ways from Parliament.[7]

Supporters of the Forward Movement also believed that Methodism had been much too exclusively the sect of the lower middle class.[8] They were aware that for most of the nineteenth century the leadership of the Wesleyan Methodist church had been autocratic in its methods and Tory in politics. It was said to be very difficult, if not impossible, for men of liberal views and outlook to be voted to the President's chair. Whereas both Jabez Bunting and Robert Newton had been President four times, distinguished ministers of outstanding ability but liberal views, such as Thomas Galland, MA, had failed to gain election.[9]

With a view to spreading the ideas of the Forward Movement, Hughes established and edited a new weekly newspaper, *The Methodist Times*, as a rival to the *Methodist Recorder* (founded 1861) which was considered to be too closely associated with the older generation and out of touch, both in its theology and its content, with modern thinking. The first number of the new publication appearing on 1 January 1885 stated the editor's objectives clearly in its leader, 'Our Raison d'Être':

> Hitherto evangelistic work has been too exclusively individualistic. Many devoted Christians have failed to realize that it is our supreme duty not merely to save our own souls, but to establish a Kingdom of God on earth. A Christianity which does not interest itself in politics, literature, science and art is a very imperfect Christianity. Above all we must do our utmost to promote the social welfare of the people.

There were a number of reasons why Inner London Methodism was in a somewhat sorry state in the 1880s. Anglican churches in the metropolis were often richly endowed; Methodist churches were dependent on the income from pew rents paid quarterly or annually, mostly by the better-off classes. With the dramatic improvement in suburban rail communication and the spread of the horse-drawn tramways from the 1870s, well-to-do Methodists migrated to the more salubrious suburbs. An elderly Methodist minister wrote in February 1898 that in London during the middle years of the century not even the disastrous schisms and agitation (the Fly Sheet War) had injured Methodism so much as the rush of the better-to-do classes to the new suburbs, ever increasing.[10] One somewhat gloomy view was that,

> The old chapels, with their tiers of high galleries and tomb-like pews, were deserted and repellent, beloved by ever-lessening groups of venerable saints, but to young sinners entirely unattractive.[11]

In London, Methodist practice had not departed so far from John Wesley's policy of open chapels as it had in Nottingham, where the man who was later to lead the Salvation Army, William Booth, tried to bring some ragged youths into the service by the front door, only to be told that he must take the members of his party to the back door, enter from another street, and sit them on bare benches behind, instead of facing, the preacher. But the survival of pew rents in such central London Methodist chapels as that at Great Queen Street was one of the reasons for the alienation of poorly paid labourers and their families from Methodist worship. Fred Church, who lived in the Old Kent Road, wrote that in Lockfields Chapel they had sixty members, 'nearly all poor working people most of whom found it difficult while many found it impossible, to pay ordinary quarterage and seat rent.' 'This,' he found, 'proved a barrier to effective aggressive work.'[12] Understandably, Hughes was thoroughly opposed to the pew rent system. When the West London Mission opened its doors to services in St James's Hall on 21 October 1887 there was no sign of any pews, let alone any requirement for worshippers to pay pew rents. The change of practice was made easier in so far as the Mission started the work in a *hall* rather than an already existing chapel.

To achieve his prime objective – the evangelization of the people of Inner London – Hughes believed that in certain areas Methodism would have to abandon 'the straight waistcoat of the three years system' under which a minister was obliged to 'move on' after spending three years in a circuit. Those given the task of evangelizing the great cities should, he believed, be 'emancipated from that great yoke' so that they could stay in one place long enough to have a real impact on the people.[13] Enterprise on a large scale was needed. He maintained that 'although sometimes work on a small scale was best, the new movement in London would be much more likely to succeed on a large scale'.[14]

– III –

It took over three years of persistent effort to bring the Forward Movement plans for London to fruition. The progress made can be traced in the proceedings of the Methodist Conference.

In July 1884, at Burslem, the Annual Address of the Conference to the Methodist Societies noted:

> The temporal and spiritual interests of the dense populations of our large towns, more especially of London, have excited much public attention through the year, and the subject has been thus urged afresh upon the Christian Church.

Conference appointed a committee 'to consider the subject of Spiritual Destitution in London, and to present a scheme for the consideration of the next conference'. The Chairman appointed to this committee was the Revd W. J. Brown of the Hinde Street church. It was also agreed:

> that in order to bring the densely populated and necessitous localities of London more distinctively within the scope of Evangelistic and Home Mission effort, certain districts, the spiritual needs of which cannot be provided for by the circuits to which they belong, shall be detached from such circuits, and constituted special ground for Home Mission work.[15]

A year later, at Newcastle-upon-Tyne, Conference decided to establish the London Wesleyan Methodist Mission with the object of carrying the gospel 'to such regions of London, and especially of Central London, as are most spiritually destitute and degraded'. £50,000 was to be raised by subscription over a period of five years to further this work and six trustees were appointed to administer the fund. An annual income was to be raised 'by subscriptions, donations and legacies, by grants from the Home Mission and Contingent Fund, and from the Home Mission surplusses of the three London Districts'.[16]

The reformers did not have it all their own way. They had hoped that Conference would rule that in such chapels and halls as were run by the London Wesleyan Mission all seats would be free. Instead the majority decided that 'a larger number of free seats, comfortable and easily accessible, should be provided'.[17] But this was a minor setback compared with the difficulties that emerged in the ensuing twelve months.

In the first place the grouping of circuits into Districts in the South East of England militated against the urgent consideration of the spiritual needs of the people of Inner London. The Second London District, which embraced the Hinde Street, Great Queen Street and Southwark circuits, extended south and south-east to Hastings, Brighton, Petersfield and Alton. Thus, most ministers and lay representatives attending District Committees had no experience of the problems of Inner London and had to be persuaded that the expenditure of the very large sum of £50,000 (by the standards of the time) was justifiable. In fact when the Second London District Committee met on 11 May 1886 it appointed a 'committee of advice' to consider 'cases in which the proposed action of the committee of the London Mission is deemed by any of the London circuits to be dangerous'. This was an obvious stalling device.[18] Then the unexpected decision of the committee of the London Wesleyan Mission to give priority to West London, rather than a South London, Mission, offended members of the Southwark Circuit.[19] But for understandable reasons the most determined opposition came from the Great Queen Street and Hinde Street churches.

The Circuit Quarterly Meeting at Great Queen Street on 25 June 1886, alarmed by rumours that the West London Mission would be established in Her Majesty's Theatre in Shaftesbury Avenue, resolved:

> This meeting is unanimous in its judgement that the establishment of a vast mission centre, with its manifold agencies and programme of attractive novelties, free from pew rents and sustained by the resources of the connexion on any site east of Piccadilly Circus, would result in the absorption of all that part of the congregation that resides west of the chapel, including many young people in West End houses who are zealous workers in connection with the Sunday School and mission band.
>
> It is obvious that the loss of such a large proportion of the congregation and society would involve the chapel trust and the circuit in financial difficulties . . . Whatever success might attend a mission centre in the neighbourhood of Shaftesbury Avenue it would be obtained very largely at the expense of the congregation and society of the Great Queen Street Chapel.[20]

Four days later the Circuit Quarterly Meeting at Hinde Street resolved that:

The locality for a West End centre suggested by the Committee [of the London Wesleyan Methodist Mission] touches immediately on the neighbourhood in which many of our families and young people live. The north-west boundary of the area desired by the Committee is scarcely more than half a mile from the Great Queen Street Chapel. The innovating character of the services proposed to be held in the mission centre, the absence of pew rents . . . the infectious irregularity which must for a long time obtain with regard to class contributions, and the constant round of pleasing religious excitements would make such a mission a powerful and dangerous rival to the established circuit agencies of Methodism.[21]

In the meantime the Committee of the London Wesleyan Mission had invited Hugh Price Hughes to undertake the superintendency of the West London Mission and he had accepted on condition that the Revd Mark Guy Pearse should be appointed to help him in this work. The Revd Mr Pearse agreed 'most heartily' to these plans.[22]

The final stage of the struggle to establish the West London Mission was reached at the Methodist Conference held in London in July 1886. At the Pastoral Session on Friday 30 July the Revd W. S. Brown of Hinde Street called the scheme for the London Wesleyan Mission 'a fiasco – an ignominious and notorious failure'. The proposal was 'premature and ill considered' and he did not wish 'to join in producing another fiasco'.[23] At the Representative Session on 3 August Dr Osborn of Cambridge reflected the views of those who were apprehensive of Hugh Price Hughes's radical approach. He said: 'This appointment would not command my confidence and would not in my judgment be the best adapted for the work which the brother will have to do.' He then expressed the very understandable concerns of the Society at Hinde Street:

> Are they not going tomorrow to lay the foundation of a new chapel in Hinde Street? Did they not contemplate an outlay of £15,000? . . . I do not think it is the part of wisdom to destroy work we have carried on at so great a cost.[24]

Both Hinde Street and Great Queen Street circuits had memorialized the Conference urging delay in establishing the West London Mission. Hugh Price Hughes answered the various objections to the plan for a mission both in the columns of *The Methodist Times* and on the Conference floor. He claimed that if the West End centre were established it would be 'not a rival but a powerful ally of the Hinde Street and Great Queen Street circuits'. His opponents were under a misapprehension.

> Some condemn the West End mission on the ground that it is Mr Hughes's proposal; but as a matter of fact he has had no more to do with the scope and character of the London Mission than the Man in the Moon. The programme of the Mission was elaborated by the London ministers' meeting when Mr Hughes was resident in Oxford. And the West End mission in particular was devised in the Executive Committee of which he was not a member.

In the light of Hughes's consistent advocacy of the London Mission in *The Methodist Times*, many of those present at Conference, no doubt, took those statements of his with a pinch of salt. However, there was no gainsaying his most important argument:

> Here in the West Centre was a vast district four miles long and two miles broad, stretching from Great Queen Street in the east to Warwick Gardens in the west, and from Hinde Street in the north to Westminster in the south, with a population of 400,000 in which Wesleyan Methodism was unrepresented except for two or three small mission rooms.[25]

The Conference minutes record that the resolution in favour of establishing the West London Mission was carried 'by a large majority'. Hughes called it 'An epoch-making Victory'.[26]

3

The Early Years of the West London Mission

– I –

In his Introduction to the *First Annual Report* of the Mission in 1888 Hugh Price Hughes wrote:

> The West End of London is the most important sphere of Christian work in the British Empire, and therefore in the world.[1]

Read at the distance of a century this statement seems presumptuous, almost arrogant. It would not have seemed so to many at the time. The point is that Hughes believed it and, believing it, brought to the task of founding the Mission the single-minded zeal and unbounded energy which were the hallmarks of his character.

Although the Wesleyan Methodist Conference had voted decisively in favour of the creation of a large mission in London's West End, Hughes still needed to convince many in the church that priority needed to be given to that part of the capital. The London Wesleyan Mission had already established the East London Mission in 1885 and the Central London Mission (at Clerkenwell) in 1886. Both needed money. It was also pointed out that since the setting up of the Metropolitan Wesleyan Chapel Building Fund in 1861, £600,000 had been spent on building large chapels in the Greater London area.[2] However, these chapels were generally constructed in the more prosperous suburban areas; the inner city was still very inadequately provided. Hughes maintained that the case for concentrating on the West End was that 'physical suffering was more intense, though less extensive' than it was in the East.[3] The 'Sisters of the People', employed by the Mission, were shortly afterwards to confirm that people in the neighbourhood of Poplar were 'better fed and healthier' than the 'thin, pale, sickly' poor of Soho.[3] The 1891 Census showed that overcrowding, i.e. in excess of two persons per room, was greater in Holborn (56.5%) than it was in Whitechapel (55.5%).[4] The reason for this state of affairs was that in the West End rents took a larger slice out of the meagre incomes of the poor than they did in the East.

In the interim between the Conference decision of August 1886 and the opening of the Mission in October 1887, Hughes and Pearse were very busy raising money for the new venture and explaining its purpose to Christians throughout the length and breadth of the country. In November 1886 they conducted a campaign in Newcastle; in January of the following year they were in Birmingham; by the end of March they had visited both Manchester and Nottingham. Following a huge meeting in the Exeter Hall, London, the total raised reached £20,000.[5]

At Newcastle Hughes said that he considered the site of Her Majesty's Theatre in London's Haymarket was eminently suitable for the headquarters of the Mission since it was 'right in the centre of the Devil's kingdom'.[6] But when it was discovered that a rent of £6,000 a year was being demanded the idea had to be dropped. Eventually St James's Hall, on the north side of Piccadilly, near to the Circus and with entrances from both Piccadilly and Regent Street, was secured for Sundays and Fridays only at a rent of £1,200 a year.[7] That this prime site was made available at relatively small cost was due to the fact that for over twenty years it had been used by an evangelistic society originally sponsored by Lord Shaftesbury (1801–85). The Society's committee took the generous view that the Mission might have more success in evangelization than it had done.[8]

When Pearse and Hughes began their work together they were (apparently) given free rein to fix their ministerial stipends. According to Pearse the matter was settled in the following conversation:

HPH   We are our own stewards. We can appoint our own salary. What shall we take?

MGP   Well, it is for you to settle that. You must remember that it is your livelihood. You might be making £10,000 a year if you had chosen to go to the bar (*laughing*).

HPH   Well, let us take £200 a year all told.

The house and furniture in each case was provided by the Mission.[9]

Pearse's reason for stressing that it was his colleague's livelihood was because they both knew that sales of Pearse's devotional books, estimated at between four and six million, brought him a comfortable income. Hughes's £200 a year might be compared with a labourer's £50, or a craftsman's £100–£150.

It was also decided that they would live within the area they were serving. Thus, on completion of his three-year stint at Brixton Hill, Hughes and his family moved to 8 Taviton Street, WC1. The large majority of the Mission's full-time workers lived either 'over the shop' or within walking distance of it.

Hughes's aim was to bring people to Christ. He was not concerned to sponsor a denominational crusade. He stressed that the organization was to be 'on a catholic basis' and he was glad to report that the Mission enjoyed the co-operation of members of all Christian churches.[10]

– II –

This was one of the reasons why the famous Baptist evangelist C. H. Spurgeon was invited to conduct the opening service of the Mission at 11.00 a.m. on Friday 21 October 1887 in the St James's Hall. Since the seating capacity was 2,500, there was understandable nervousness as to whether the hall would be filled, particularly as the service was being held on a weekday morning. In the event the bold experiment was fully justified, and the hall was full.

The regular programme of Sunday services began two days later. In the morning service at eleven o'clock Guy Pearse dealt mainly, but not exclusively, with the personal aspects of Christlike Christianity; but he abhorred 'other-worldliness'. Rather the aim was to qualify men and women to do the work of Christ on earth. At three o'clock the Mission brass band struck up to attract an audience for Hugh Price Hughes's 'Conference' which was said to be conducted on the French plan in which Hughes, on his own admission, 'did all the conferring'![11] Here the stated purpose was 'to deal separately, systematically and permanently with the social effects of the teaching of Christ'. Jesus was held up 'as the author of social as well as individual salvation'.[12] An orchestral band of fifty instrumentalists played to a crowded hall from 6.00 to 6.30 p.m. before the start of the evening service, conducted by Hughes on strictly individualistic and evangelistic lines. This pattern of activities was followed throughout the year, except that the afternoon conference was discontinued through the months of July, August and September.

The response from the public was tremendous. Within a year of the opening of the Mission, every Sunday evening all 2,500 seats of St James's Hall were filled long before the service started. Because, on occasions, as many as 2,000 persons were turned away at the doors, the Princes' Hall, on the opposite side of Piccadilly, was hired, and overflow services were conducted by the Revd Dr Henry Lunn, who joined the team of ministers in 1889. In the *Third Annual Report* Hugh Price Hughes wrote of Sunday congregations numbering 'upwards of 5,000 people'.[13] The number of church members organized into classes rose quite remarkably from 123 in 1888 to 1342 in 1893.[14] In April 1888 it was decided that to give 'outsiders' an opportunity to attend services in the crowded halls, 'regulars' should be requested to stay away once a month. It was a move which succeeded in bringing more of the poorer members of the community in touch with the church.[15]

The Superintendent and his assistants were prepared to innovate if this would bring people in to hear the message of the gospel. Mr Josiah Nix, who first met Hughes in the Methodist Church, Oxford Circuit, borrowed the military terminology of the Salvation Army. He organized 'Public House Brigades', 'Praying Brigades' and even a 'Fire Brigade' whose members wore a red ribbon and were 'willing to go anywhere and do anything when called upon in the name of Christ and Humanity'. To advertise the activities of the Mission, Nix hired a furniture van and used a magic lantern to display notices on a large screen attached to the back. A horse then drew the van through the streets of Soho and Belgravia.[16]

For the Sunday evening services in St James's Hall the orchestral band accompaniment was the main innovation, but on one memorable Harvest Festival Hughes installed a live sheep in a pen below the pulpit. Unfortunately, the sheep's bleatings interrupted some of the preacher's 'purple passages'. The experiment was not repeated.[17]

– III –

In the summer of 1887 when they were planning the work which was to start that autumn, Hughes and Pearse conceived a division of labour between the morning and evening services. Hughes wrote to Pearse: 'You would edify the saints and I would pursue the sinners.'[18] In this way they would hope to reach both those who could lay claim to be Christians and those who had had little contact, if any at all, with the Christian church. Undoubtedly the main purpose of establishing the Mission was to reach out to those many thousands, particularly the materially and spiritually impoverished, who inhabited the slum warrens between Oxford Street and Piccadilly. In his famous survey *Life and Labour of the People of London*, Charles Booth claimed that the poor and desolate who were helped during the week by the social workers of the Mission were not the ones who filled the seats in the St James's and Princes' Halls on Sundays.[19] Hughes himself conceded that 'the morning congregation consisted largely of young men and young women from the great West End houses of business. It is also frequented by earnest seekers after saintliness.'[20] Outstanding in those days, before the introduction of khaki as standard wear for uniforms, were the red coats of soldiers who were alloted a part of the gallery on the right-hand side of the preacher. In the same gallery were seats reserved for policemen, dressed in plain clothes. A special place in the gallery facing the preacher was set aside for hospital nurses in uniform.[21] The audiences for the Afternoon Conferences which varied in number between 1,500 and 2,000 comprised a great majority of men and included a preponderance of those in steady work.[22]

However, before rushing to the conclusion that the Mission largely failed in its objective of bringing the gospel to the poor, it would be wise to look at *all* its evangelistic activity. The mistake of Booth was to concentrate his attention on what might be called the show-pieces of St James's Hall and Princes' Hall. He was right in finding there, besides the young men and women of the Great West End houses 'well-known habitués of West End Clubs, keen-eyed journalists and men about town'. But the Mission soon had other centres of activity more withdrawn from the limelight than the two halls in Piccadilly and less off-putting to the reticent, poor unbeliever. When space was needed for members' classes, for administration and for the organization of social work it was found in the Wardour Chapel in Little Chapel Street on the south side of Oxford Street. This had been a flourishing Congregational chapel, but the migration of Oxford Street tradesmen to the suburbs had sadly depleted its numbers. The Revd Andrew Mearns placed the building at the disposal of the Mission. The pews were removed, new chairs installed, and the building renamed Wardour Hall. The rooms were reorganized. It is indicative of the ecumenical outlook of Mearns, Hughes and their churches' members that it was agreed that the large Congregational Sunday School should continue to use

Wardour Hall, Little Chapel Street (now Sheraton Street)

the building and that adult congregations should merge. The management of the new centre was left largely to Mr Nix and his assistant the Revd W. T. Piper. Services or meetings were arranged for every day of the week, including Sundays. Prominent features of the work included orchestral concerts on Saturday evenings and lantern lectures on Thursday evenings. Included in the repertoire of the latter were such topics as 'Niagara', 'Cromwell', 'Ireland', 'Our teeth: how they come' and 'Our teeth: how they go'.[23] By these diverse means more people of the immediate neighbourhood were drawn into the life of this community church. It was reported that in the first year alone there were five hundred conversions. These were far more likely to be persons of humbler social status than the converts who came forward to the enquiry rooms after the services in the two Piccadilly halls.

Cleveland Hall, Cleveland Street

In 1889 a new branch of the Mission was opened in Cleveland Hall in Cleveland Street, half-way between Tottenham Court Road and Great Portland Street. In the 1850s the hall had been erected by the Secularists of West London and had been crowded with men and women anxious to hear the speeches of Charles Bradlaugh, Annie Besant and G. J. Holyoake. Later in the century it became a dance hall before the lease expired and the building was left to deteriorate. The Mission needed to spend over £1,000 to make it habitable again. As was the case with the Wardour Hall, there were Mission activities every day of the week. In the immediate vicinity there was 'a perfect warren of human beings', many in a semi-destitute condition. But whether it was through the innovation of the coffee bar, the lantern lectures or the services (or a combination of these), a church community was established – one suspects largely of poorer people – so that by 1893 membership reached 328 and over one hundred of the keenest were organized into six classes.[24]

Through the initiative of Lady Henry Somerset, who owned the land in the district, the Chalton Street Hall, in Somers Town, just north of Euston Road and near the great railway terminals of Euston, St Pancras and King's Cross, was opened on 3 October 1892. The hall, which was a small one, was purposely built under the supervision of the Revd Barlow Sargeant, who succeeded Dr Lunn as a full-time minister of the Mission in 1890. Besides the

The People's Hall, Chalton Street, Somers Town

mission hall, the building included a street-level coffee bar, class rooms, a dispensary, and residential accommodation for several of the Mission's Sisters. Here the social work received greater prominence, but nevertheless many of the poor families of the district took an active part in the services held in the hall.[25]

In 1894 the Wardour Hall had to be demolished, and the ground landlord would only re-let the site at a greatly enhanced rent. Once more the Congregational Church came to the rescue. It allowed the Mission to use the Craven Chapel and Craven Hall in Fouberts Place, 206 Regent Street. Though the staff had regrets at leaving 'Old Wardour', the new premises were more commodious than the old, so that twice as many services and meetings as before and more classes could be held. Thus it proved possible to bring still more of the poor of Soho under the influence of the Mission.[26]

– IV –

The rapid expansion of the work of the Mission in the first few years of its history added greatly to its capital outlays and operational expenses despite the fact that a number of its activities were self-supporting. In the first full financial year to 31 March 1889 total outgoings amounted to £8,441. 4s. 3d. To offset these expenses offertories raised £2,567. 5s. 11d.; subscriptions and donations produced £4,443. 10s. 10d.; advances from the general treasurers yielded £1,195. 19s. 3d., while the remaining balance came from young people's services and from funds carried over from the 1888 accounts. There were over a thousand subscriptions and donations, from the £500 given by a well-known wealthy Methodist of the day, to 'A Soldier's Daughter's' one shilling. More varied and numerous were the gifts in kind. Most common were parcels of clothing, though sacks of peas, onions, turnips or apples, bundles of blankets,

Craven Hall, Fouberts Place

21

parcels of toys and bunches of flowers, including '37 bunches of primroses', were included. The well-known coal merchant, J. Corry, presented ten tons of coal; Mr Joyce sent meat 'two or three times a week'; Messrs Scales and Son gave forty pairs of new shoes. Others sent in large quantities of currants and raisins. These gifts greatly aided such work as running soup kitchens, providing workhouse teas, provisioning the Christmas dinner and the Sisters' relief of destitution. Clearly the Mission was greatly dependent on the goodwill and financial and other material support of thousands of people for the continuance of its work.

– V –

How is the outstanding early success of the West London Mission to be explained? The answer lies partly in the imagination and inspiration of the leadership. Hugh Price Hughes and his team understood much better than did most of their contemporaries the needs and aspirations of the people of West London, many of whom lived in drab and impoverished circumstances. Hughes saw that in the 1880s the music hall had eclipsed the theatre in popular favour. He concluded that if the church was to gain adherents it must offer music, a hopeful gospel and warm and friendly surroundings. There were impressive performances from either the choir, the brass band or the orchestral band at each of the Sunday services, and the weekday concerts were of an exceptionally high musical standard.·

Many shop assistants of the big West End establishments lived in dormitories above their place of work but were locked out on Sundays after breakfast until ten o'clock at night. Before the Mission was established, a writer in the *Wesleyan Methodist Magazine* observed that for shop girls Sunday was a 'dreadful problem'. Some of them walked about the streets or sat in parks; some could be traced 'going from church to church to find one which was warmed'.[27] To many St James's Hall and Princes' Hall must have been regarded as welcome places of refuge.

Few people living anywhere in the territory bounded by Oxford Street, Charing Cross Road, Piccadilly and Hyde Park can have been unaware of the existence of the Mission. Apart from Mr Nix's publicity efforts, open-air services were held not only in Hyde Park but on a daily basis in the side streets near the mission halls.

This was a time when worshippers, but especially the men,

largely judged the value of a service by the quality of the sermon. R. Mudie-Smith, who conducted a religious census of London in 1903, maintained that the outstanding lesson of the census was that 'the power of preaching is undiminished'.[28] More than 10,000 people thronged the Tabernacle in Southwark at one or other of the Sunday services each Sunday in 1886 to hear the great preacher C. H. Spurgeon. Within a few years of his death in 1892 the congregation was down to 3,600.[29]

Hugh Price Hughes was not a great preacher in the Spurgeon tradition of finely tuned eloquence. One critic said that he was not an outstanding preacher in that 'he had little imagination and most of his sermons were topical rather than expository'.[30] But perhaps it was that very topicality and relevance to the concerns of his time that made his appeal to his huge congregations. He won over at least one influential convert because he taught that 'the interests and the social needs of the people were an integral part of the teaching of Christ'. His 'unselfish, chivalrous enthusiasm for the oppressed' was what captivated her.[31] He had a strident, rather than a mellifluous voice: but his hearers were carried away by his burning sincerity and by their understanding of the simple, but profound, truth of his message that Christ's love extended to *everyone*.

The fervour which Hughes brought to his sermons permeated the Christian community which he led. The spirit of unity amidst diversity of talents was achieved in the Friday evening devotional meetings held in the Princes' Hall. Hughes's belief that this was the 'pivot around which the whole Mission turns'[32] would have commanded general agreement.

Finally, there was the work of the 'Sisters of the People' who met the lonely, the sick and the troubled face to face in their own homes. Their work was so important that it merits treatment in a separate chapter.

4

The Sisters of the People

In the first half of the nineteenth century most daughters of well-to-do parents in England were educated by governesses at home. The emphasis of teaching was on accomplishments such as needlework, singing and the pianoforte rather than on academic subjects. Nevertheless, as the century advanced, opportunities for the higher education of women opened up. Colleges for women were founded in Oxford and Cambridge in the 1870s, augmenting the facilities already available in the University of London. However, professional employment opportunities for women were extremely limited, since, in a male-dominated society, the prevailing belief was that woman's proper sphere of activity was in the home. The frustration experienced by educated young women of the middle and upper classes was forcibly expressed by Olive Schreiner, who achieved fame through the popularity of her novel *The Story of an African Farm* (1883). In her less well-known book, *Women and Labour*, she wrote:

> In that clamour which has arisen in the modern world, where now this and now that is demanded for and by large bodies of modern women, he who listens carefully may detect, as a keynote beneath all the clamour, a demand which may be embodied in such a cry as this: *Give us labour and the training which fits for labour! We demand this, not for ourselves alone, but for the race.*[1]

Katherine Price Hughes had great sympathy with these views. In her youth she had been 'tremendously impressed' on hearing speeches by Mrs Garrett Anderson and Mrs Fawcett advocating more opportunities for the higher education of women and their employment in the professions.[2] In her autobiography she recalled the time which she and her husband had spent in the Brixton circuit before the West London Mission was established:

> I wondered if it were possible to form some organisation which would reach the educated young women of our own church. I thought especially of those who were not obliged to earn their own living and who remained at home . . . with practically nothing to do and simply longing to have some outlet for their energies, and a purpose in life.[3]

The idea of a Sisterhood took shape one day when she was reading a life of Joseph Mazzini. When she came to the chapter which related how the Italian patriot founded the society 'Young Italy', the members of which were pledged to their country's liberation, she thought of harnessing the youthful idealism of the women of Protestant England to further the idea of human solidarity and brotherhood. Young Italy had the rallying call 'For God and the People': she would organize the 'Sisters of the People'.[4]

Mrs Hughes was familiar with the work of the Methodist Children's Home founded by the Revd Thomas Bowman Stephenson in 1869. In 1871 Stephenson visited some of the battlefields of the Franco-Prussian War and was greatly impressed by the work of Pastor Theodore Fliedner of Kaiserwerth, on the lower Rhine, who organized his uniformed deaconesses to care for the wounded. On his return to England Stephenson decided to call the women on his staff 'The Sisters of the Children' and to dress them in a distinctive uniform. There were further precedents in the Sisterhoods of the Roman Catholic and Anglican churches and in the women officers of the Salvation Army. In America the first deaconesses in the Methodist Episcopal Church were organized by Mrs Lucy Ryder Meyer of Chicago in 1887 – the same year in which the West London Mission was founded.[5]

– II –

Hugh Price Hughes gave a clear indication of the kind of women he and his wife hoped to recruit to the Sisterhood when he wrote in one of the early reports of the Mission:

> I must beg special attention to Mrs Price Hughes's appeal for more Sisters. What ladies of leisure, culture, refinement and devotion will volunteer for this most blessed work?[6]

The response to such appeals was very gratifying. In 1893 Mrs Hughes wrote that she was 'overdone with applications for entrance into the Sisterhood'.[7] From three recruited to the end of 1887 the number of Sisters rose swiftly to forty in 1894. Thereafter there was a decline, and then a levelling off, to between twenty and twenty-five in the decade before the outbreak of the First World War. The main problem was not lack of recruits but shortage of funds to provide more accommodation and to finance the relief and rescue work. At first no payment was made to the Sisters; but by 1907 a minority received 'small salaries in addition to their board and lodging'.[8]

There is no doubt that those recruited to the Sisterhood were 'ladies of leisure, culture, refinement and devotion'. The first to be enrolled was Sister Katherine Page of Walmer Court, Kent, who devoted fifty years of her life to the work of the Mission before being obliged to retire through ill health. In the late 1890s she was the first woman to be elected to the Westminster Board of Guardians. A number of the women, including Sister Hilda Tindall, daughter of the Revd William Tindall, and Sister Clara Holden, had been scholars at the same high-class school, Daleham, as had been attended earlier by Mrs Hughes. Sister Lily, who took charge of Katherine House, the Sisters' residence, first at 19 Montague Street and later, from 1891, at 10 Fitzroy Square, came from the prosperous Dewhurst family of Bradford.

While some Sisters devoted the greater part of their lives to the work of the Mission, others moved on to marriage, or to other forms of social welfare activity in London and further afield. Sister Agnes emigrated in 1892 to undertake relief and mission work amongst the poor of Capetown. Sister Ada Vachell's Christian and humanitarian endeavours in the West Country are commemorated in a tablet in Bristol Cathedral. Sister Kathleen Fitzpatrick, who displayed a special aptitude in caring for children, later took charge of Lady Henry Somerset's Children's Colony at Duxhurst. She then turned her hand to writing children's books and lives of the Australian explorers.[9]

Among the ablest of this very distinguished group was Sister Emmeline Pethick, who, in the summer of 1890, when she was twenty-three years of age, wrote to Mrs Hughes from her comfortable home in Weston-super-Mare, expressing a desire 'to get in touch with working girls and share with them'. Her letter was acknowledged. A few weeks later she received a telegram urging her to come to London as soon as possible to take the place of Sister Mary Neal, who had been in charge of the Girls Club, but had fallen sick. Miss Pethick took the train to London on the following morning and began 'an entirely new life' with the Mission. A month later Mary Neal returned and the two struck up a lasting friendship. By 1895 they had become increasingly dissatisfied with the institutional life at Katherine House, which they considered too far distant from the homes of the very poor they were supposed to help, and they chafed at the orthodox Methodists' opposition to drama and dancing (with which they had hoped to attract the allegiance of the members of the Girls Club). When they requested permission to rent a small flat of their own in the midst of the slums of Soho, Hugh Price Hughes frowned upon the suggestion. They therefore resigned from the Mission and shortly afterwards set up a women's co-operative dressmaking establishment, Maison Espérance, in Wigmore Street, where the employees were paid a minimum wage of fifteen shillings a week – roughly twice the sweated labour rate then prevalent in the trade – and where orders were received from 'fashionable women who were interested in the condition of those who made their costumes'. The two women were trying to put into practice 'the gospel of Socialism as it was preached . . . by Keir Hardie'. In 1901 Emmeline Pethick married Frederick William Lawrence, who shared her ideals and supported her stand when she was imprisoned as a suffragette in 1906 and 1909. He was himself imprisoned in 1912 at the same time as she was once more in custody, this time being forcibly fed. Emmeline ended her career as wife of a cabinet minister when in 1945 Clement Attlee appointed her husband (by then Lord Pethick-Lawrence), Secretary of State for India.[10]

Meanwhile, Mary Neal, in association with Cecil Sharp, played a big part in the revival of English folk song and dance and was joint author (with Frank Kidson) of a book on this subject in 1915.[11]

– III –

That all these women found so much scope for the exercise of their talents was in no small measure due to the enlightened liberal attitude – on most questions at least – of their 'Sister Superior', Mrs

Hugh Price Hughes. When she was asked why the term 'Sister' was used, she replied that it was intended to express 'a truly human relationship as in the sight of God, and not as an ecclesiastical position'.[12] Applicants were interviewed by the Mission Superintendent and their appointment had to be confirmed by the Executive Council after a three-month probationary period had been served, mainly in 'room to room' visiting. The uniform, as shown worn by Sister Lily in Plate 10, was obligatory. Margaret Bottome of the New York *Christian Advocate*, who visited the Mission in 1889, described it as follows:

> Their dress is uniform – black serge, with white linen collars and cuffs. The long grey veil is what distinguishes them; it is put on the bonnet in folds and hangs down the back.[13]

The purpose of the uniform was to make the Sister easily identifiable when on duty before and after Mission services or when making visits to those in need. The style of the uniform was changed after the First World War for ease of maintenance and to match the headdress more nearly to the style of the 1920s.

The Sisters were not required to take a vow, nor was it regarded as essential that they should be Methodists. The purpose of the Mission was to bring people to Christ, not to proselytize. Converts were encouraged to join their local church, of whatever denomination. Hence Baptists, Quakers, Anglicans, Congregationalists and Presbyterians were all to be found in the Sisterhood at different times.

Beyond the requirements of wearing the uniform, residing in Katherine House or one of the other buildings of the Mission and reporting weekly to the Sister Superior, the Sisters were left as free as possible to do their own work in their own way. The policy adopted from the beginning was clearly stated by Mrs Hughes:

> We try in every case to encourage individuality and never to repress it. Whenever a Sister shows a special aptitude for one particular branch of work, we let her devote herself to that, leaving her unfettered to organise and accomplish her ideas, of course holding her responsible for the conduct of the work in harmony with the spirit and aims of the Mission.[14]

The Mission welcomed help from those women who did not feel

able to devote their whole time to its work. These 'part timers', or auxiliaries, lived at home and were known as Out Sisters.

— IV —

Hugh Price Hughes described the Sisterhood as 'by far the most important departure of the Mission'. However, the activities of its members were so varied and numerous that I shall divide them into two categories, the first of which may be broadly classified as pastoral and evangelical whilst the second embraced social welfare work foreshadowing the creation of the Welfare State. The first category will be considered in this chapter and the second will be the subject of the chapter which follows. Inevitably these divisions are somewhat arbitrary since there was a great deal of overlapping, but they may, nevertheless, be helpful.

There was nothing haphazard about the requirement that each probationer sister should spend most of her time in district visiting. Within the area served by the Mission there were thousands of men and women who were in physical or mental distress. Thousands more were lonely and friendless. After ten years of visiting the homes of the neighbourhood, Sister Katherine came to realize 'that it was an immense comfort to these poor people to find someone to listen to them'.[15] Sister Emmeline believed that the secret of being a Sister was 'to enter into a home and into a life so quietly that the kinship that you claim becomes silently accepted'. One day when she was having a little talk with the mother of one of the girls' club members there came a knock at the door.

'Come in, come in,' she answered. 'Come in, Mrs Smith' (as the neighbour seemed to hesitate at seeing me). 'There ain't nobody here; leastways there's only Sister, and she ain't nobody, as you may say.'

I could not help feeling what a grand thing it is to be a nobody . . . When you are a nobody other people give you their best and truest because they give you themselves.[16]

What won the hearts of the people was that the Sisters treated all they met as equal in the sight of God. One woman who was dying of cancer said, 'It is worth dying, Sister, to be treated so like a lady.'[17] The Sisters were prepared to put their hand to anything from bandaging an injury, to sweeping the floor or cooking a meal, as well as reading from the Bible. One of them who visited a starving woman in the slums of Soho took advantage of her absence from her room for a while to cook her a substantial meal. When the woman returned to her cheerless home and her empty cupboard she found waiting for her what she described as 'such a treat'.[18]

Sisters were present at all the services conducted by the Mission, not only in the principal centres of St James's Hall and Princes' Hall, but also in the smaller meeting places such as the Wardour, Cleveland and Craven Halls. After services they helped in the Enquiry Rooms to which members of the congregations resorted to ask about church membership or seek help in the solution of their many problems. They took charge of many of the weekly devotional classes. In 1910, for example, thirteen of the Mission's classes were under the leadership of Sisters.

Fifty teenage girls of the Soho neighbourhood were invited to attend the first meeting of a Girls' Club on 10 April 1888. The plan was to provide some activity between 8 and 10 p.m. every evening except Saturdays and Sundays. A number of Sisters took it in turn to be in charge. At the close of the first meeting 'the girls all seemed to be desperately amused at being requested to kneel down, and when a short prayer was offered they all simply roared with laughter'. Mrs Hughes reported that on another occasion 'three or four rather big or coarse girls started dancing' which was 'against the rules and never allowed'. When a reinforcement of more Sisters was called in to clear the hall the girls lay down on the floor.[19] The climax came some months later, the situation being described by Sister Mary:

> After a general stampede in which chairs were thrown about, the boards of the floor lifted where the gas is laid on and the bell rung until I could not hear my own voice, I turned them all out and next morning went round to consult Mrs Hughes.[20]

She said that managing the club was the work which God wanted her to do, provided she could be given a free hand to do it. Mrs Hughes wisely consented. Starting fresh, Sister Mary 'expelled the worst girls', but took them back one by one after a private interview. A year later she wrote: 'We have so gained the affection and confidence of the girls that we can do with them what we will.'[21] So much had their attitude changed that when she asked whether they would like to have a short evangelical service each week, every girl voted in favour. The programme included two evenings a week for 'sewing, reading and quiet games' and Friday evenings when there was 'singing and any game they like'. Dancing was taboo; but on those evenings when 'rhythmic exercises' were on the programme something uncommonly like it was to be seen. In Sister Mary's view the Girls' Club was not designed simply to keep troublesome teenagers out of mischief. She saw such ventures as a 'training school for working women who will be instrumental in the very near future in altering the conditions of the class they represent'. To this end she organized discussions on a wide range of subjects including 'trade unions; General Booth's plan (for old age pensions); penny novelettes; temperance; sweethearts; street organs; dancing(!) and dress'.[22] Before she left the Mission she tried to get the girls 'to form a committee from among themselves to govern the club instead of the paternal government which had hitherto been in vogue'. But it was of no avail. The girls' answer was always the same: 'We love the Sisters and the Sisters love us. What more do we want?' Maybe the words inscribed on the star-shaped badge they wore – 'Love faileth never' – had given them this idea.[23]

Many of the mothers of the teenagers in the Girls' Club attended the first Mothers' Meeting of the Mission held on 8 November 1887 when no less than 300 women were present. Meetings were from 2.30 to 4.30 one afternoon a week and the women came for the companionship, warmth, needlework instruction and illustrated talks that were provided. There were occasional outings to the nearby countryside in the summer months.

As they walked to and from St James's Hall and Princes' Hall in Piccadilly the Sisters became all too familiar with the extent of prostitution in the area. One of their number, Sister Margaret, determined to try to mitigate the evil. Dressed in her uniform, she walked up and down Piccadilly between midnight and 2.00 a.m., when solicitation was at its peak, to give the women the opportunity to get in touch with her. She found there were 'none, or very few, who were there because they wanted to be there'. In graphic terms she described the problem:

> Without a character, encumbered with a child, who would give them work even supposing work was to be had? The pure flame of mother love awakened in their hearts demanded above everything else that the child should be provided for. They could endure much, but they could not endure to see a baby pine and starve. The way of escape

was at hand (the descent to it is made very easy). No helping hand was near, so they went down and sold themselves, body and soul, to help the child.[24]

Mrs Hughes believed that what was needed was a home for the rehabilitation of the women; but it was not until February 1893 that sufficient money was raised to buy and furnish Winchester House in Walthamstow ready to admit the first residents. The house

Winchester House, Walthamstow

was named after the city which was the home of Canon and Mrs Butler, who devoted their lives to the rescue of prostitutes.[25] In 1898 the house was sold since it was regarded as being too far distant from the centre of London. In its place a home was opened up 'within walking distance of Piccadilly Circus'.[26] In 1909 Hall Caine, the novelist, gave the Mission a small flat near Leicester Square to which the Sisters could take the women they had managed to contact in the streets.[27]

The poor people's loathing for the workhouse was well understood by the Sisters. As far as resources would permit they tried, in 'deserving' cases, particularly the elderly, to provide small allowances to enable an independent existence to be continued. To those who were already workhouse inmates entertainment, games – such as musical chairs – and refreshments were provided once a week when they were allowed outside the workhouse walls. From the St Marylebone Workhouse they went to Cleveland Hall, from Poland Street they were welcomed at Craven Hall, and from St Pancras the venue was Somers Town. Those who were too sick to leave the workhouse were visited once a week.[28]

To many of the poor the prospect of getting a job depended partly on their appearance when interviewed. To improve their chances, Miss Page of Walmer Court set up the Sheen Society in the Spring of 1888, the object of whose members was 'to make and collect garments for distribution amongst the poor who live in the districts visited by the Sisters'. Local branch secretaries in different parts of the country undertook to collect and send off the garments to the Mission at least once every quarter.[29] In 1893 a second-hand goods depot, mainly for second-hand clothing, was opened in a house at 160 Wardour Street. In the following year another depot was opened at the Cleveland Hall, Cleveland Street. For the best part of eighty years the Mission maintained a depot or depots of this type.

Sister Grace, like many of her contemporaries, had read Mrs Ewing's book *The Story of a Short Life: or Laetus Sorte Mea* (Happy in my lot), and she was familiar with Mr Ready to Halt, in Bunyan's *Pilgrim's Progress*, who was resolved 'to run when I can, to go when I cannot run, and to creep when I cannot go'. Whatever befell, he was 'going on a pilgrimage'. From the experience of these readings the Sister determined to establish a guild for the mentally and physically disabled. In 1895 the regular monthly teas of the 'Guild of the Poor Things' were started. In the intervening weeks the members of the Guild were visited by the Sisters in their own homes.[30]

It was not until he wrote his annual report for 1895 that Hugh Price Hughes was able to record that the Mission had a Sunday School of its own in Soho. The reason for the late start was partly that there was already a flourishing Congregationalist Sunday School in the area, as well as the Methodist one in Hinde Street just north of it, and it was only in that year that two new Sisters were enrolled with a positive genius for work among children.[31] Thereafter the Sunday Schools went on from strength to strength.

– V –

In surveying the first ten years' work of the Mission, Hugh Price Hughes admitted that there had been 'one great conspicuous omission and failure'. They had not succeeded in establishing a Brotherhood.[32] The *First Annual Report* in 1888 noted that there were nine young men 'Brothers' living at Lincoln House and that they conducted open air meetings in the evenings. However, eight of the nine had full-time jobs in London. Only one of the nine, a man of independent means, devoted the whole of his time to the Mission. Subsequent *Annual Reports* make no mention of any organization of brothers. The explanation must surely be that whereas the situation for middle-class women was as described at the beginning of this chapter – a hunger for useful work to do – for middle-class educated men there was no lack of job opportunities.

– VI –

It might appear from this outline of some of the Sisters' activities that there was a one-way traffic in benefits, that the staff of the Mission were giving up a sheltered life to help the less fortunately placed members of society living in the tenement dwellings of Soho and neighbourhood. This was certainly not the whole story. The Sisters learned a great deal from the experience of their life among the poor. When Sister Cecilia began to specialize in caring for the sick, some of her preconceived notions were shattered:

> The causes of illness among the poor I am not so much disposed to attribute to drink as many are . . . the want of suitable food and ventilation (the latter especially at night), aggravated by their circumstances and mode of life will account for much of it.[33]

Emmeline Pethick-Lawrence, writing from the perspective of the late 1930s, recalled 'how restricted in the last decade of the nineteenth century were the lives of the girls of the middle class'.

> The very idea that women should leave their homes and live in the comparative freedom of a community in order to carry out rather subversive principles of social sharing was a bombshell to the large mass of conservative, low church Nonconformist opinion.

Of her debt to Katherine Price Hughes she wrote:

> She gave me my first experience of that emancipation of mental and

Hugh Price Hughes 1887–1902   C. Ensor Walters 1902–07

J. Ernest Rattenbury 1907–25   C. Francis Ream 1925–6

1.   Superintendents of the West London Mission

Ira Goldhawk 1926–36   Donald Soper 1936–78

John Newton 1978–86   Leslie Griffiths 1986–

2.   St James's Hall: interior

3.   St James's Hall: the Piccadilly entrance

4. Mark Guy Pearse and Hugh Price Hughes, 1896

5. Slum boys, 1899

practical powers which is to be found by working as free persons in a community of equals, and, though I did not realise it at the time, my first interview with her . . . was a beginning for me of a new life of the spirit.[34]

Martha Vicinus summed up what must have been the experience of many of the Sisters of the People when she wrote:

A Sister or Deaconess sacrificed a great deal of personal freedom in return for a community that helped her to overcome her failings and supported her as completely as any family could. Through community work she gained self-development and self-knowledge. Life within a religious community at its best was a living example of the Christian paradox that to lose one's life for others was to gain it.[35]

5

The Social Work of the
Mission before 1914

– I –

A fortnight after the opening of the West London Mission Hugh Price Hughes devoted his Sunday afternoon conference in St James's Hall to the subject 'Jesus Christ and Social Distress'. 'The time has come,' he declared, 'when we must pray God to give us grace to discharge our duty in public as well as to say our prayers in private.'[1] Three weeks later, speaking in the same hall on the subject 'Jesus Christ the Greatest of Social Reformers', he declared, 'Jesus Christ came into the world to save human society as well as to save individuals. Indeed, you cannot effectually save the one without saving the others.'[2] After Hughes's death on 17 November 1902, his immediate successors in the office of Superintendent, C. Ensor Walters (1903–7) and J. E. Rattenbury (1907–25), were of like mind. In the Mission's journal *Advance*, Walters wrote, 'Jesus came not merely to save the individual, but to found a kingdom ... Let us beware lest, notwithstanding our national profession of religion, the judgement of God fall upon us because of our national neglect of justice to the poor.'[3] Preaching in the Lyceum Theatre, J. E. Rattenbury spoke even more bluntly when he declared that 'if Christians are born again without a hatred for social evils and enthusiasm for the establishment of a new order, they are born again blind'.[4]

The social welfare schemes sponsored by the Mission from its foundation were prompted by these beliefs.

– II –

It was not until 1955 that the term 'Welfare State' appeared in the *Oxford English Dictionary*. It was then defined as 'a policy so organized that every member of the community is assured of his due maintenance with the most advantageous conditions possible for all'. By 1914 it could not be said that the West London Mission served so comprehensively the needs of the people living within its geographical area – its resources were far too meagre to enable it to tackle more than the fringes of the problems of poverty and distress. But the list of services provided at that time is impressive in its range. It included the running of a crèche for the infants and young children of working mothers; the organization of numerous youth clubs; the relief of unemployment through the provision of job registries for both men and women and a labour yard for men; the servicing of dispensaries and surgeries and the maintenance of a system of health visiting; convalescent home treatment for those recovering from sickness or in desperate need for a rest and change; the manning of a 'poor man's lawyer' service and the maintenance of a 'Home of Peace for the Dying'. The Sisters of the People played a key rôle in all these activities; without their Christian dedication to the work none of the schemes would have stood any chance of success. Many of the ventures were pioneering ones which blazed a trail for subsequent municipal or state action.

– III –

The credit for establishing the first crèche in London belongs to a Quaker woman, Marie Hilton, who shocked many Christians when she opened what became known as Mrs Hilton's Crèche, at 16 Stepney Causeway on 22 February 1871. Her critics maintained that mothers should be the sole custodians of their children and that they were guilty of neglecting their responsibilities if they left them to the care of others while they went out to work. In any case, the very word 'crèche' aroused suspicions. It sounded very foreign. Marie Hilton was undeterred by these detractors. In the summer of 1870 she had been greatly impressed when visiting a crèche in Brussels where over 500 children, whose fathers had been killed in the Franco-Prussian War, were given loving care by a team of nurses and teachers. Back in England she answered her critics: 'They did not know that in starving East London the women had to work equally with the men to provide food for the children.' In Whittingham's 1557 translation of the New Testament the word 'cretche' was used where other translators used the word 'manger'. Mrs Hilton wrote that 'in Belgium the word crèche or manger . . . was adopted by the originators in remembrance of the babe of Bethlehem having lain in a manger, and thus they were endeavouring, by their loving care of the little ones, to re-echo the blessed song of peace on earth and good will to men'. In 1888 the

Lincoln House, Greek Street

Stepney Causeway Crèche was visited by, among others, 'the ladies of the West London Wesleyan Mission, to whom very ample information was given'.[5]

In that same year 1888 Mrs Hughes arranged that a crèche which had been opened in the previous year by the Hon. Maude Stanley and other ladies should be transferred to the West London Mission and accommodated in Lincoln House, 60 Greek Street, Soho.[6] She never had the least doubt about the importance of this undertaking. In 1893 she wrote:

> Nearly all the mothers of the children who come to the nursery are compelled, through various causes, to be the bread winners of the family, and the crèche has thus not only proved a benefit to the women but an unspeakable blessing, both physically and morally to the little ones.[7]

For four years from 1888 Sister Katherine had responsibility for the running of the crèche along with other duties; but from 1892 the gifted Sister Hope, who was not only professionally qualified but also greatly attached to young children, was able to give its management her undivided attention. She stayed in the job for over thirty years. There was never any need to advertise the facilities on offer. Working women who found that Sister Hope and her staff looked after the children very well told their neighbours and friends and there were always plenty of applications. Sometimes the other Sisters, in the course of their house visits in the neighbourhood, would encounter situations of desperate need where the admission of a child to the crèche would make the difference between life and death. In February 1892 Sister Jeanette was approached by a widow whose little boy, aged two and a half years, had measles and bronchitis. She had just been offered a job, but if she turned it down in order to look after her boy, both mother and child would starve. No hospital would admit an infant with measles. So the Sister asked the poor law authorities to take the boy in the infirmary for a fortnight, only to be told that this would only be possible if the mother entered the workhouse with her son. Thwarted in every direction, the Sister arranged to visit the one-room tenement home three times a day to give the boy nourishment while his mother was at work. When the measles crisis was over, the widow brought her child daily to the crèche where he was bathed, clothed, fed and taught until she collected him in the evening and paid the daily charge of four pence to Sister Hope.[8]

From its original home in Lincoln House, described as 'incredibly difficult to keep clean',[9] the crèche was moved to more spacious and airy accommodation in the Craven Hall in 1895. The final move was to the sixth floor of Wesley House, Kingsway, in the summer of 1911, where the Mission crèche remained for seventy years until taken over by the Greater London Council.

Average occupancy was between forty and fifty children a day. Even after they started to attend the local Board School the children would return to the crèche for a mid-day meal and again in the evenings to await the arrival of their mothers.[10]

The fourpence a day paid by the mothers covered only one-third of the cost of running the crèche. The rest Sister Hope raised partly from the proceeds of an annual sale of work held in the spring; partly from the endowment of cots at £5 a year; partly from the contributions of the members of a Daisy Guild, each of whom agreed to contribute a guinea a year, and partly from other small contributions.[11]

In pre-1914 days at least, working-class women and children were the chief beneficiaries from the crèche. The mothers worked as charwomen, laundresses, tailoresses and office cleaners or were employed in pickle factories or seed merchants' warehouses and shops.[12]

The important contributions made by the crèche to the well-being of the poor of Soho and district was revealed on those rare occasions when it was necessary to close its doors to some of those most in need. In 1894 there was an epidemic of measles. In the *Annual Report* of the Mission Sister Hope wrote:

> The little children! How they suffer! . . . An epidemic of measles; the crèche doors closed to those who were suffering. What are the consequences? The mother ceases her work, there is little or no coal, little or no food. The tiny frames cannot fight against such ills, so day by day, one after another dies, until when Christmas comes the registers record sixteen deaths.[13]

– IV –

In late Victorian and Edwardian times unemployment was sometimes a very serious problem in London's West End. In 1892, 1894, 1903 and 1908–9 thousands depended on emergency relief to keep them from starvation. The clothing trades which occupied many of the tenement dwellers were notorious for the seasonal and casual nature of their employment, so that even in years of nominal prosperity large numbers suffered severe distress in slack seasons. Arthur Sherwell, who worked for the Mission in the mid-1890s, reported that the winter of 1894–5 was one of 'unprecedented severity and depression'. He found that families 'whose thrift and industry were beyond reproach' were found in rooms 'destitute of furniture and fire and food'. From Cleveland Hall alone '450 soup tickets a week were distributed to people whose cases had been carefully investigated'.[14]

Within a year of its foundation the Mission opened up a men's labour exchange. In the second *Annual Report* Hugh Price Hughes commended the work of Mr Nix, who had been 'very successful in getting good and permanent employment for men out of work'. Its importance lay in demonstrating the need for such an organization and for showing what might be done on a larger scale by municipal or state action, rather than in the size of the operation – fewer than one hundred men were found jobs in the first year. Meanwhile, at Lincoln House Sister Mary kept a servants' registry, open on Wednesdays and Saturdays from eleven till one, with the object of helping the girls in the Mission's classes to obtain employment in Christian families. She also kept a cupboard of suitable clothing to help those taking up domestic employment to have a more presentable appearance.[15]

While he was in charge of relief work in 1895–6, Arthur Sherwell organized a wood chopping 'factory' at Cleveland Hall where unemployed men were given work a few weeks at a time at trade union rates. When Sherwell left the service of the Mission little was done to maintain the experiment. But in 1905, encouraged by the Mission's new Superintendent, C. Ensor Walters, the Revd C. Copeland-Smith, one of the assistant ministers, brought new energy to the task and broadened the scope of work provided in the factory. A house adjoining Cleveland Hall was leased to provide more space, and firelighters, saucepan stands, knife boxes, plate racks and door mats were made, besides the ever-popular bundles of firewood. An average of fifty men were employed each week. In the first fifteen months of the new management over 10,000 men were interviewed, and the copious personal records compiled by the staff filled 2,000 pages in six large quarto volumes.[16]

– V –

Howard Barrett, Katherine Price Hughes's brother, received a medical training at Edinburgh University before taking up a practice in the East End of London in the 1870s. He was horrified at the ravages caused by starvation, smallpox and cholera among the poor in the docklands area and resolved to do something practical to alleviate the suffering endured by the underprivileged in London society. However, he saw that he would need capital to enable him to take up philanthropic work and he therefore 'betook himself to more westerly and less afflicted regions'.[17] By the time the doors of St James's Hall were opened to services in October 1887 he had established a lucrative practice among the wealthier classes of the West End. Within a year the Medical Department of the West

London Mission was in operation with Howard Barrett as its Honorary Superintendent.

From the start Barrett had fully qualified Sisters to help him with the huge task of caring for the sick poor. In his first report the Medical Superintendent stated: 'We shall not go to the expense of a dispensary of our own'; but the local chemist proved to be unreliable and in 1889 the Mission's own dispensary was set up at the medical headquarters at Lincoln House. Two years later it was found essential to establish a second dispensary in the Cleveland Hall. Mr Barrett was available for free consultation in his surgery at Lincoln House every Friday morning, and in the winter and spring was assisted by Dr Lunn, who came on the Wednesday mornings. But the greatest service was rendered by the Sisters, who visited hundreds of poor people in their own homes. They were the key link in the chain which sometimes ended in the doctor's surgery, sometimes with escorting the patient to hospital with an invaluable 'letter of admission' donated by a hospital subscriber to the West London Mission, and sometimes with arrangements being made for the patient to enter a convalescent home, again with the aid of the previous letter of admission. An average of over 650 cases a year were visited in the first three years of the medical department. Sister Cecilia, the first of the qualified nurses to be employed, noted that the Mission supplied her with inhalers, steam kettles, air cushions, bed rests, blankets, bandages, material for poultices, babies' clothes and a medicine chest. Sadly, all too often she was dealing with the symptoms rather than the causes of illness. In his second annual report Mr Barrett wrote: 'I found that the malady from which a very large number of the poor applicants for my advice and medicine were suffering was Hunger.'[18] Sister Cecilia's experience was similar: 'To those among the sick whose improvement depends upon suitable food – and they are a great majority – I take beef tea.'[19]

From 1890–8 the Mission ran its own convalescent home, donated by a sympathizer: Wesley House, Bisley, near Stroud, Gloucestershire, where residents stayed for a fortnight or a month 'as necessity demanded,' at a cost of twelve shillings (60p) a week with full board. Up to a hundred debilitated or physically or mentally exhausted persons were helped towards recovery each year. After maintaining the home for nearly eight years it was decided that, in view of the distance of Bisley from London (107 miles), and high overhead costs in running the establishment, it would be better for the Mission to concentrate on other more urgent work.[20]

The work of the nursing sisters was made harder because of the attitude of the Poor Law authorities to destitution and sickness, which, it was often held, arose from the improvidence and thriftlessness of the poor, who had to be persuaded to do better through the dread of the workhouse. A very real stigma attached to the workhouse and Poor Law Infirmary before 1914. In 1909 Beatrice Webb (and others) exposed the iniquity of the system and the way it aggravated the problems of the sick poor.

> It has been demonstrated . . . beyond all dispute that the deterrent aspect which the medical branch of the Poor Law acquires through its association with the Deterrent Authority, causes, merely by preventing prompt and early application by the sick poor, an untold aggravation of disease, personal suffering and the reduction of the amount of producing power of the industrial working class.[21]

In 1894 Sister Esther noted:

> To go into an infirmary one becomes a *pauper*. Once I advised a hard working man to call in the parish doctor because he could not afford to pay for one.
>
> He said, 'Oh Sister, that means I shall be considered as a pauper!'
>
> I said, 'Surely not. You work when you are well enough and you are not going into the infirmary.'
>
> He took my advice, but the next time I visited him I saw that on his bottle of medicine was written the shameful word 'Pauper'. I crossed it out and wrote 'Patient', a course I always intend to pursue.[22]

The absence of any system of National Health Insurance caused great distress to the sick poor whose incomes were not large or regular enough for them to subscribe to private insurance schemes. Sister Jeanette asked a woman whose daughter was dying of consumption how long it was since her daughter had left off working. The reply came, 'About a week'. When the Sister probed further: 'But how could she do her work when she must have been so ill?', the mother answered: 'She knew that there was nothing coming in except what she earned, so she had to go on working as long as she was able.'[23] It was experiences such as this which made the Sisters welcome the National Insurance Act of 1911 which introduced a system of contributory health insurance for those earning less than £160 a year.

Howard Barrett was of the opinion that although London was much better endowed with dispensaries and hospitals than most other British cities it lacked adequate provision for the dying poor. He discovered that:

> Under unavoidable circumstances, and in an extremely large number of cases, the respectable and self-respecting poor in their last illness and death in this Nineteenth Century of the Christian era, had no choice but to suffer as best they could, under conditions of great misery and degradation.[24]

After two years of searching for a suitable property, the West London Mission's St Luke's House (Home of Peace for the Dying) was opened by Lady Battersea at 50 Osnaburgh Street, Regent's Park, on 14 July 1893. In the wards there were six or seven beds for men and eight or nine for women. The home was managed by Howard Barrett as Medical Superintendent – he relinquished his superintendency of the Mission's Medical Department to Heywood Smith so that he could give his undivided attention to the new venture – with a matron, two or three nursing Sisters, and domestic staff.

Howard Barrett said that St Luke's was a home 'where respectable but well nigh destitute poor . . . can retire to die in decency and

St Luke's House, Osnaburgh Street

comfort.' The home was open to people of all denominations or none, but it was not open to all and sundry regardless of character. One of the questions asked on the admission form for St Luke's was: 'Has he or she ever been in receipt of parish relief or an inmate of a parish infirmary?' If the answer was yes, it had a 'very disqualifying effect'. No charge was made to patients, but next of kin were expected to pay the cost of removal and burial.

Howard Barrett made St Luke's an attractive last home for its residents. Every window had its outside box of marguerites and geraniums; the wards were brightly painted and decorated with an abundance of flowers. Most importantly the doctors and nurses were by no means glum. 'We are usually cheerful and have many pleasantries and jokes among ourselves,' Barrett reported. This was in sharp contrast with other contemporary 'hospices' where patients were put straight to bed on admission and generally kept there. They were given neither dressing gowns nor slippers, had no outdoor clothing and were only allowed visitors for half an hour in the evenings. It was a death-house image. In St Luke's, on the other hand, the patients considered themselves very fortunate to spend their last days in such a happy atmosphere. They appreciated particularly the solace brought by the saintly Mark Guy Pearse, who was the chaplain.

In 1901 it proved necessary to relocate St Luke's to two houses in Lawn Road, Hampstead. When a speculative builder who was at work on the opposite side of the road discovered its purpose, he considered it would depreciate the value of his property, and pulled strings to have Howard Barrett and his staff evicted within less than a year of their arrival. It was eighteen months before a move was possible, to a fine property at 14 Pembridge Square. Twenty years later, in 1923, it moved again to Hereford Road just round the corner.[25]

The Mission ceased to be involved with St Luke's in 1911, but Howard Barrett continued as Superintendent until 1914 when he handed over the management to his son. The Christian spirit of the house and the principles of its management continued long after the Barretts had left.[26] The example of St Luke's remained, greatly to influence developments in the 1970s and 1980s. In 1948 Cecily Saunders went to St Luke's as a volunteer registered nurse, and remained for seven years, thoroughly imbibing the philosophy and method of administration of the house. In 1967, by which time she had become fully qualified as a doctor, she founded St Christopher's Hospice, Sydenham, London, acknowledging fully the debt she owed to Howard Barrett and his voluminous annual reports on St Luke's. Between that date and 1980 no less than fifty hospices, based on the pattern of St Christopher's, were established in Great Britain. In the humane treatment of the dying poor the West London Mission had undoubtedly led the way.[27]

In 1907 infant mortality in the slum area of Somers Town was 232 per 1,000 compared with a London average of 130. Through the initiative of members of the Bunting family, Dr Barrett and others, a St Pancras School of Mothers was established in that year. The West London Mission made the basement and ground floor of the Chalton Street premises available for the new venture, and the sign 'Mothers and Babies Welcome' was displayed over the entrance. At the school a weighing machine for mothers and babies was provided, demonstrations and lectures (some illustrated) on all aspects of baby care were given and information about food, cooking and health care was freely available.

The Mission connection with this valuable enterprise ended in December 1908 when new premises were acquired in 37 Chalton Street. The importance of the initiative can be gauged by the fact that 218 babies under one year of age were brought to the school by their mothers in the first ten months of its existence. The story of the school is told in *A School for Mothers* written by Evelyn and Dora Bunting and others and published in London in 1907.

– VI –

In the tradition of John Wesley, Hugh Price Hughes was keen that lawyers, as well as doctors, should give free advice and aid to the 'deserving' poor. In the summer of 1880 he preached at Ripley, Derbyshire and stayed the night with Thomas Slack, a prominent local Methodist, who introduced him to his son, John. Hughes's interest was roused when he was told that the young man was training for the law; in return John was attracted to the minister's ideas on the proper rôle of Methodism in society. After he had qualified and practised in Derbyshire, John Bamford-Slack – as he was now known – came to London in 1889 and soon took an active part in the affairs of the West London Mission. In 1892 he started a

Poor Man's Lawyer service each week from Lincoln House. To those who were unable to pay solicitors' fees he gave free advice on such diverse matters as compensation for injury, the resolution of domestic disputes and the unfair eviction of tenants. When he was returned as a Liberal MP in a bye-election in Mid-Hertfordshire in 1904 some of his partners took over the duties of Poor Man's Lawyer. After Bamford-Slack died at the comparatively early age of fifty-one in 1909, the service gradually faded out.

– VII –

Hugh Price Hughes's theology was simple and Christ-centred. He wrote that 'Jesus Christ was essentially a man of the people – a working man: the laws and policies of states must be subjected to the teaching of Jesus Christ.'[28] He was perceptive enough to realize that if the church ignored the need for political reforms the work of the West London Mission would be stigmatized as a mere palliative, staving off the demand for more fundamental changes in society. In his Introduction to the Mission's *Annual Report* of 1899 he wrote:

> Of course the great social problems cannot be solved by any individual or any Mission. There must be an appropriate division of labour between Church and State. The Church may, in a few instances, set an example and teach the State how to do its duty; but the social aspect of the problem must be grappled by the state itself.

He supported the organization of trade unions, particularly of women, to enable wage earners to push their earnings above the disgracefully low levels which ruled in the tailoring and dock workers' trades. He was on holiday in Switzerland when the great London dock strike took place in the summer of 1889. Dr Lunn preached to both morning and evening services at St James's Hall on Sunday 1 September, choosing his morning text from Acts 17.26: 'And hath made of one blood all nations of men for to dwell on the face of the earth.' The dockers were on strike to back a demand that their wages should be raised from 5d. to 6d. an hour (the 'Docker's Tanner') and that they should be guaranteed four hours minimum employment each day. Dr Lunn cabled Hugh Price Hughes, asking his permission to take a collection for the dockers' families. 'Mr Hughes at once wired an affirmative reply, saying his sympathies were entirely with the strikers.'[29] In November of the same year one of the Mission's class leaders, Mrs Sheldon Amos, called a great meeting in Charrington's Great Assembly Hall in East London. Mr Hughes appeared on the same platform as the famous Labour leaders John Burns, Ben Tillett and Clementina Black, and a Woman's Trade Union Association was formed. In the *Annual Report* for 1889 Hughes wrote:

> There can be no effectual remedy on a large scale until women workers combine and organise to abolish starvation wages. Multitudes of poor women are now compelled to work for one penny an hour, and their day of toil often extends over sixteen and even seventeen hours.[30]

Hughes also believed that Christian discipleship should also be expressed by membership of Parliament, local authorities and Boards of Guardians. He welcomed John Bamford-Slack's election to Parliament in 1904 and rejoiced when his fellow minister C. Ensor Walters was elected to the St Pancras Vestry in 1897 and re-elected at the head of the poll as a councillor, following local government reorganization, in 1900. As Chairman of the Public Health Committee, Walters carried through a scheme for the demolition of slum properties and their replacement by municipally owned 'model dwellings'.[31]

In 1894 Sister Edith (Gresham) was elected as a St Pancras Guardian of the Poor. When she stood for re-election she, too, emerged at the head of the poll. Many of the electorate had a great affection for her since she had served them unstintingly as a Christian Sister.[32]

6

The Open Air Witness

– I –

The tradition of open air evangelism in England is as old as the history of the English church itself. It is recorded that when St Augustine came to Thanet in AD 597 to convert the Jutes and Saxons to Christianity, it was at an open air meeting that he brought the good news of the gospel to King Ethelbert.[1] At critical times in the subsequent history of the church, reformers resorted to the highways and fields to appeal over the heads of those in authority, to the common people. Thus in 1380 John Wycliffe created an Order of Poor Preachers to take the Bible truths direct to the peasants and craftsmen. In 1548 the Protestant Bishop Hugh Latimer preached at St Paul's Cross – less than a mile away from the spot where the Revd Donald Soper began his weekly meetings on Tower Hill in 1927 – denouncing abuses within the church and in society. He deplored the fact that, 'Whereas in times past men were full of pity and compassion, now there is not pity, for in London their brother shall die in the streets for cold.'[2] The tradition of open air preaching has been particularly strong in Methodism. On 31 August 1739 John Wesley preached to 'eight or ten thousand people' on Kennington Common.[3] On another visit to the capital on 10 October 1756, he preached to 'a huge multitude in Moorfields' and afterwards wrote in his *Journal*: 'It is field preaching which does the execution still; for usefulness there is none comparable to it.'[4]

– II –

This must also have been the view of Josiah Nix, Hugh Price Hughes's Organizing Secretary, for the *First Annual Report* of the West London Mission, published in 1888, includes a photograph of him preaching to a crowd of people in Hyde Park. However, open air meetings were not confined to 'Speakers' Corner', as that part of the park nearest to Marble Arch came to be known. At that time the side streets of Soho were not crowded with vehicular traffic, so that it was possible to hold meetings close to the tenement dwellings where thousands of people lived. Nix reported that:

> At the sound of the cornet and the harmonium up go the windows and often quite a hundred people will be listening from the houses and many rush into the streets.[5]

A favourite location for Saturday evenings was at the corner of Betterton Street and Drury Lane since this was half-way between a betting shop and a public house 'whose swinging doors were hardly ever closed'. A soprano soloist helped to attract an audience on these occasions.[6]

Nevertheless, for Sundays, Hyde Park was the best place. On any fine Sunday afternoon from May to September 'there were at least 200,000 people who pass up and down one path between 6.30 and 10.30'.[7] The large majority of these people did not attend any place of worship. R. Mudie-Smith, who, in 1904, edited the findings of a *Daily News* religious census of London, noted that even in those areas of the city where a high level of church attendance might have been expected, 'the majority of the inhabitants remain[ed], owing to either indifference or hostility, uninfluenced and untouched'. Posing the question 'How are these to be reclaimed?', he answered: 'There is only one way; since they will not come to us, we must go to them, and go to them with our best and not our feeblest.' The religious revival of the eighteenth century, he reminded his readers, was due to John Wesley's open air preaching.[8]

The activists of the West London Mission, aided from time to time by the Mission Superintendents, W. Ensor Walters and J. Ernest Rattenbury, took this lesson to heart. For several years on Sundays during the summer months they held all-day services at which there would be as many as twenty-one different speakers, mostly local preachers recruited from the 700 local preachers then living within the London area.[9]

The great enthusiast in the years before the First World War was Thomas Wicks, who spent the first seven years of his adult life as a trooper in the Cape Mounted Rifles, before returning to London and falling under the spell of Hugh Price Hughes. *Advance* reported that 'though he lived a toilsome life, Sunday was his hardest working day of all'. When he died early in 1915 he had completed twenty-five years as an open air preacher in the park.[10] The typical arrangement of the open air campaigns in the early days was for those taking part in the services to be led in procession by the Mission brass band from Soho to the park. Addresses by a succession of speakers would be interspersed with the singing of hymns, the words of which were displayed in large print on a stand next to the speaker's rostrum, the music being led by a harmonium. For many years Patience Gatridge was the soloist at the services organized by Thomas Wicks. Meanwhile, other helpers handed out 'Decision Cards' to members of the public, and each Sunday some of these were handed in when the proceedings ended.

C. Ensor Walters, who was Superintendent of the Mission from 1903–7, was a great believer in the value of open air exposition of the Christian faith. At the Methodist Conference in Liverpool in 1912 he moved,

> That at the May Synod in its Representative Session each circuit shall be asked 'What is being done to secure effective open air work within its boundaries?'

and further moved,

> That training in open air work be part of the curriculum in the training of theological students.

Both these resolutions were adopted by the Conference. He also edited *The Open Air Speaker's Handbook* which was published in London in 1914 under the direction of the Home Mission Committee of the Wesleyan Methodist Church. George Allen, the Superintendent of the Leeds Mission, in a chapter entitled 'The Preparation of the Speaker' recommended 'Physical exercises, moderately and wisely directed, the open window, the cold bath, the light but sufficient food and the avoidance of late hours' as the right form of training for the job.

Although the form of the meeting was generally that of an act of worship, this did not deter some members of the crowd from interrupting the preacher. Walters's book contained a section entitled 'How to deal with the heckler', in which W. H. Armstrong wrote: 'Experience proves that the typical heckler has not a great variety of questions.' This view was confirmed at a later date by Donald Soper, who found that the questions posed by his audiences could be grouped into just three main categories: criticisms that the Christian church did not live up to its ideals; issues raised by recent political developments; and the challenges made by scientific discovery to the established tenets of Christianity.[11]

The size of the Hyde Park audiences varied greatly from year to year and from season to season. 1905 was an exceptionally good year because large crowds came to London to visit the Great Exhibition at the White City. Since it was found that attendances fell away sharply in the winter months, it was at first customary to close down operations in mid-September until the following May. In 1907, however, it was decided to continue both afternoon and evening services 'as long as the weather was at all fit', and that winter there were only two Sundays on which they were cancelled.[12]

Another tradition established in the first decade of the new century was the celebration of harvest festival. Members of the crowd were warned in advance of the date and were invited to bring fruit, vegetables and flowers to place at the foot of the rostrum on harvest thanksgiving day. To the 1907 festival fifty bunches of grapes and a lot of baskets of fruit were brought. A year later friends at the Regent Street Polytechnic and many others were thanked for 'providing a beautiful display of flowers and fruit' which went to St Luke's House and to the Sisters for distribution to the sick and needy.[13]

In the first year of the Great War concern was expressed that it might not be possible to continue the Hyde Park activity. The July 1915 issue of the Mission's magazine *Advance* noted:

> We have begun our open air services, but we have to deal with the universal difficulty. Our men have gone to the front. Our last young man has enlisted, and, consequently, we have to carry our pulpit, harmonium and hymn stand ourselves, or leave them at home.

However, under the direction of J. P. Holloway, renewed zeal was brought to the task; services continued throughout the winter of 1915–16, and for the spring of 1916 a comprehensive series of evangelistic addresses was provided, the theme being 'The Kingdom of Jesus Christ as a Model of Practical Politics'. The following syllabus was issued and followed through the enusing weeks:

1. The fundamental idea
2. Structure and constitution
3. Legislation and administration
4. Domestic policy
   (a) as affording social responsibility
   (b) art and literature
   (c) science
   (d) trade and labour
5. Foreign policy
6. Attitude to war.[14]

For the remaining months of 1916 and 1917 the work in the open air appears to have flourished as never before. In the summer of 1916 and in the following winter 'almost daily meetings' were held. A flexible approach was adopted as the meetings proceeded, 'Now by song, now by question, now by testimony, now by sermon'. A base for the participants was secured at 12 Old Quebec Street, just behind the Marble Arch tube station. In these rooms the workers were given training through Bible study and discussion and refreshments were provided. A Hyde Park Society with a peak-time membership of 200 'Hydeparkers' was established.[15] By 1917 *Advance* noted the establishment of a system of 'Guards'. London was divided into thirty-five districts with a 'Guard' responsible for the 'Hydeparkers' resident in each. For some months a strong *esprit de corps* was established. Thereafter, the activity faded out almost as rapidly as it had blossomed.

The explanation of the decline in the open air witness lies partly in the intensification of German air raids which 'greatly affected attendance' in the Mission's churches;[16] partly through the absence due to illness of the Superintendent J. E. Rattenbury between October 1917 and September 1918, and partly through the extension of the West London Mission circuit at the end of 1917 to include the Hinde Street and Warwick Gardens chapels.[17]

It is arguable that after the war conditions were less favourable for maintaining the same pattern of outdoor Christian witness as had existed earlier. The horrors of trench warfare, the loss of nearly a million young British soldiers in the often senseless slaughter of no-man's-land, the scandal of profiteering at a time of shell

shortages and the cynical character of the Versailles peace settle-
ment in 1919 made many of those who survived the disasters of
war far more critical of Christian teaching and practice. When the
Mission was founded in 1887 there was no popular daily press,
and it was only gradually after the sensational and cheap *Daily
Mail* appeared in 1896 – 'a penny paper for one halfpenny' – that
newspaper reading spread more widely among poorer families. By
the 1920s, however, the habit was well established and many were
supplementing the information gleaned from the press by listening
to the radio broadcasts of the BBC. There were other counter-
attractions to the religious service, whether conducted out-of-
doors or within walls. In the inter-war years more than twenty
million people visited the cinema each week. Thus the Hyde Park
meetings continued through the 1920s and 1930s, but on a much
reduced scale.

– III –

In the meantime, however, a very different type of open air
Christian advocacy had been started in another part of London.
1987 marks the centenary of the foundation of the West London
Mission, but it also marks the diamond jubilee of Donald Soper's
lunch-hour meetings on Tower Hill. Although these meetings
began before his appointment as Superintendent of the West
London Mission in 1936, they continued throughout his leadership of the Mission, and have continued to the present day. It is
therefore appropriate to refer to them here.

The occasion for the start of this prolonged adventure of faith
was a conversation with a young City worker in the congregation
of the South London Mission in Old Kent Road where Soper was
serving as Methodist probationer. During week-day lunch hours
this young man went to Tower Hill, where he heard the speakers
of the Catholic Evidence Guild as well as advocates of the Protestant fundamentalist standpoint. He felt that much religious propa-
ganda on Tower Hill was a waste of time since it did not relate to
the experience of the listeners. He challenged his new minister to
'have a go' and do better. The challenge was accepted, and one
Tuesday afternoon in the summer of 1927 Donald Soper mounted
the wall overlooking the Tower and faced the verbal onslaught for
the first time.[18]

According to Douglas Thompson there are two ways of preaching the Christian message. The one most commonly used, and certainly used by the West London Mission before 1936, was 'to proceed from Jerusalem to Jericho, from the place and symbol of religious doctrine and observance, to the arena of everyday life'. The other approach, from Jericho to Jerusalem, was that taken by Donald Soper, because he believed this was Christ's method.

> For Jesus the gospel lay in a woman breaking bread, a farmer scattering seed, a Prince going to seek a kingdom, a slave-master fiddling his accounts. These were the gossip points in Jesus's world.[19]

In one of his seemingly extravagant statements he asserted that,

> though it is not important that the preacher should have any basic philosophy of life if he ventures into the open air, it is of the utmost importance that he should have read the newspaper . . . If the speaker in the open air has not attended the headlines, he will be written off as an ass.[20]

In fact Donald Soper *did* approach the Tower Hill meetings with a basic philosophy of life. It was that,

> If all things cohere in Christ (as Paul declared), then it must be true that one can begin at any point which itches in any mind, with a question which comes from any of the disciplines of human thinking, and end up in the Christ-centred pattern of all things.[21]

The open air speaker, then, was well advised to have a clear idea of his starting point – probably an issue much in the headlines at the time – but thereafter the content of the meeting would be largely determined by the questions raised and interjections made by members of the crowd. The speaker should *use* the question, and not merely answer it. In this way the relevance of the gospel can be brought home to the audience. The kind of speaking appropriate to the open air is 'of the staccato variety', with no long and intricate sentences. The members of the crowd come and go, so that each sentence should contain something of note.

Of course there are great risks in this kind of advocacy. The speaker must be prepared to face any kind of question or interjection. There is no possibility of retreat 'to the dungeon of the pulpit or the escape hatch of the vestry'.[22] Questions can be both disrespectful and irreverent, as when one heckler asked: 'Who washed up after the Last Supper?' Quick repartee and a lively sense of humour are invaluable as these will win over the crowd. But answers can be hurtful as well as amusing. An atheist objected to the speaker's reference to 'feelings of the heart'. He said, 'The heart is not an instrument of feeling. It is a pump. That's what the heart is.' The speaker suggested that the questioner was unmarried, and when the reply came that he was, indeed, unmarried, the speaker turned to the crowd and said that he knew why this was the case. There had been an occasion when the young man had been in love and had said to his beloved 'I love you with all my pump.' She turned him down.[23]

Donald Soper recognized that the open air meeting had 'perceptible and recognized limitations'. It was a 'pro-ministry or pre-ministry' providing a 'shop window' for the Christian approach. If you win the sympathy of at least some people in the crowd, through the fact that you are willing to stand up and be challenged on any issue, and through your good humour and obvious enjoyment of the cut and thrust of argument, you break down barriers, if you are convincing and sincere, and then it will be less difficult for those who hear you to take other steps which elsewhere will be offered.

Many a member of the Kingsway Hall congregation had first heard the Christian message in the open air. One unobtrusive member of the crowd on Tower Hill lost his wife in childbirth. He had had no previous contact with a minister of religion, but he came to Donald Soper to ask him to conduct the funeral, and the friendship of the two men remained long after the agonizing experience of the loss of a loved one had passed.[24]

– IV –

In the 1920s and 1930s Donald Soper sometimes joined students from Richmond College in conducting open air meetings in Hyde Park. At that time the crowds were almost exclusively British or European; there were very few black or coloured persons to be seen. Rather than having to compete with the exponents of African nationalism, as was the case in the 1950s and 1960s, the Mission speakers of those days had to vie with such outstanding characters as Bonor Thompson, described as 'the pewkiest wit I ever enjoyed who could talk about anything or nothing with consummate skill', and the masterly and saintly Father Vincent MacNab.[25]

Donald Soper's regular Hyde Park meetings began in the spring of 1942. During the preceding six months he had been discussing with some of the keenest members of the Kingsway Hall church a 'basic ration' of five key points of the Christian gospel. At the last of these meetings he suggested that it was time for them to proclaim their faith, and that he would take his stand in Hyde Park in the afternoon of Passion Sunday. He asked his audience to support him by their presence and, if they felt disposed, 'to try a little mild heckling'.[26] From then onwards at three o'clock every Sunday afternoon, wet or fine, winter or summer, the Mission stand would be erected and the hour-long meeting would begin. Only very exceptionally when the Superintendent was ill or out of the country and nobody could be found to take his place was the meeting cancelled.

One influence prompting the new initiative in 1942 was the decision of the Court of Governors of the BBC, early in 1941, to exclude from all access to broadcasting prominent persons who were known pacifists. These included Dr George MacLeod of Iona; Canon Charles Raven, the Emeritus Professor of Divinity at Cambridge; Hugh Roberton, the leader of the Glasgow Orpheus Choir; and Donald Soper. Through this action the Superintendent of the West London Mission was prevented from delivering to a large audience the very popular religious broadcasts which he had been giving since the first invitation to use this medium had come from the Revd Dick Sheppard of St Martin-in-the-Fields in 1934.[27]

7

Years of Turmoil

– 1 –

In the first sixteen years of its history, guided by the single-minded zeal of Hugh Price Hughes, the work of the Mission expanded rapidly. Despite the absence of a permanent headquarters, a mood of confidence and hope prevailed. The following sixteen years, by contrast, were punctuated by crises in the leadership and by difficulties in finding a suitable centre for the activities of the church. This chapter could well have been headed 'Mission in search of a Home'.

On the afternoon of Monday, 17 November 1902, Hugh Price Hughes was returning to central London from a meeting of the Christian Social Union he had attended with one of the Sisters when he dropped his umbrella on the pavement. He picked it up, but soon afterwards dropped it again. This time he was unable to recover it and the Sister, seeing that he was very ill, hailed a hansom cab and escorted him to his home at 8 Taviton Street. He was placed on the sofa in his study and died there in the presence of his family, at seven o'clock that evening. He was only fifty-five years of age. It was a great shock to all those who knew and loved him, since on the previous evening he had preached a sermon in St James's Hall with all his customary vigour. On Friday, 21 November, he was buried in Highgate Cemetery, where his last resting place is marked by a granite cross. At the service in Wesley's Chapel, City Road, which preceded the burial, the President of the Methodist Conference said:

> He recalled our early fervour and enthusiasm for the souls of men and brought us into touch with contemporary life and with great movements of the time.[1]

This was indeed Hughes's great contribution to Christian life and thought. More than eighty years after his death most Christians would endorse the message of a sermon he delivered in St James's Hall on 6 November 1887.

> We have dealt too exclusively with the individual aspects of Christian faith. We have constantly acted as if Christianity had nothing to do with business, with pleasure or with politics – as if it was simply a question of private life and prayer meetings. It is because the spirit of Christ has not been introduced into public life that Europe is in a perilous position today.[2]

Though Hughes was an ardent campaigner against social abuses and had a warm sympathy for the problems of the poor it would be misleading to call him a Socialist. As a historian of Methodism noted: 'He touched life at so many points and lived life at such a breakneck speed that consistent patient study was impossible. His thinking was influenced by Ruskin's *Unto this Last*, Lecky's *Rise and Progress of Nationalism in Europe*, and Professor Alfred Marshall's *Economics of Industry*. The writings of Marx, Lassalle and Proudhon, which were profoundly influencing European thought during his lifetime, were little more than names to him.'[3] The Revd Samuel Keeble (1853–1946), who collaborated with Hughes in the early years of the *Methodist Times*, parted company with him on matters of social policy and subsequently published *Christianity and Socialism* (1907) and *The Social Teaching of the Bible* (1909) which expressed his more radical Socialist views.

Hughes's stances on matters of foreign and imperial policy evoke less sympathy among Christians in the closing years of the twentieth century than they did in his own day. His daughter admitted that 'this democratic leader found himself a British imperialist to the fingertips'.[4] He reacted to the Bulgarian atrocities of 1877 by demanding British military intervention to drive the Turks from Europe; he supported the British occupation of Egypt in the 1880s and was strongly pro-British in the Boer War (1899–1902). A lavishly illustrated 56-page colour souvenir programme of a Sisters of the People Bazaar, held from 18–20 December 1901, reflects the views of the Mission's leadership at the time. A full-page picture of a bandaged British bulldog faces a Highland Regiment soldier with drawn sword above the caption 'Aye Ready'. Over the page, a charging cavalryman is being spirited on by a maiden in flowing robes carrying a laurel wreath. This picture is inscribed 'The Spirit of War'. The patrons and patronesses listed in the programme include a Duke, two Earls, two Lords, four Duchesses, seven Countesses, two Marchionesses and twelve Ladies. Hughes's attitude to the war was too much for Dr Henry Lunn to stomach. Though personal relations with the Superintendent were still friendly, he left the Mission to devote more time to his growing holiday business.

Nevertheless, the war fever passed and the problem of meeting the spiritual and material needs of the people of London remained. Before the Mission doors were opened for the first time, Hughes had listed 'the conditions for success' of the venture. One of these was the recognition of the fact that 'it is impossible to deal effectually with the spiritual destitution of London unless you deal also with the physical and mental destitution'.[5] His courage and determination in tackling this daunting task is his lasting memorial.

– II –

The thirty-year-old Revd Charles Ensor Walters, who succeeded Hughes, had been trained by him in the ideals of the Mission and its work. Soon after Walters left his birthplace at Milborne Park, near Yeovil in Somerset, to attend the Wesleyan Training College at Richmond, Hughes was in touch with him advising him to read the works of John Ruskin. In 1895, after graduation, he joined the West London Mission as an assistant minister. Thus in 1902 he had already worked for seven years in close harmony with the Mission's founder.

Although Walters' well girt figure and heavy gait were in sharp contrast to the slim figure and quick movements of his predecessor, his evangelical fervour was as great, though his concerns were more narrowly focussed on practical domestic issues, such as urban overcrowding and high infant mortality rates, rather than on great international issues.[6] In a series of articles he wrote for the Mission's monthly magazine, *Advance*, he commented

> It is no matter of congratulation that so many of the children of our city should be half starved and ill clothed, often falling fainting from the forms of the Board School from sheer exhaustion as the result of lack of food, in some districts 260 babies out of 1,000 dying before they reach one year in age. All these facts and many others should

give rise to serious thought and earnest resolve to alter an absolutely unnecessary state of things . . . The housing problem is bound up with the land question, and the final solution will only be found when that question is grappled with. The people must get back to the land – the land which is theirs by right.[7]

In 1900, when he was returned at the head of the poll in the elections for the newly-created municipal council of St Pancras, he had an opportunity of putting into practice some of the reforms he had advocated. He was chosen to chair the public health committee, and early in 1901 his scheme for the demolition of some notorious slums and their replacement by council-owned 'model dwellings' was given the hearty approval of the council.[8]

Walters might have done much more for better housing, child care and education had his career as a municipal councillor not been cut short through the sudden death of Hughes. His extended responsibilities as Superintendent of the Mission largely precluded these other activities. In the emergency of the winter of 1902–3 he was greatly helped by the Revd Mark Guy Pearse, who cancelled an American trip in order to help with the ministerial and pastoral duties.

The ministers and staff had scarcely time to recover from the effects of the loss of their first Superintendent when they were confronted with a major problem of a different kind. On 29 April 1904 Walters informed the Executive Committee of the Mission that the control of St James's Hall had passed to a new syndicate which planned to build a large modern hotel on the site. A new location for the Sunday services – attended, it will be remembered, by over 3,000 persons each week – had to be found at very short notice. This was the beginning of a long period of uncertainty and financial worries, when the prospects seemed to be changing almost from week to week. Walters interviewed the managers of the Empire, Palace, Shaftesbury and Hippodrome Theatres, and the Oxford Music Hall, and also negotiated with Mr Maskelyn for the use of the St George's Hall. While these negotiations were in progress the proprietors of St James's Hall suddenly offered three months' extension of the lease of the Hall until 30 September 1904. Since this was only a short reprieve, the search for alternative accommodation continued. On 15 July 1904 agreement was reached for the Sunday use of Hengler's Circus, in Argyll Street, off Oxford Circus (and the site of the present Palladium Theatre) for a rent of £800 a year, on condition that the proprietors set out the seats for the Sunday services and that there would be no lingering smell of animals at the time the congregations assembled! Two months after this expensive contract had been signed, Walters was informed that the St James's Hall could be used for a further three months, until 30 December. In consequence for some weeks services were held in both locations. In mid-December there was yet another offer: St James's Hall could be used until the end of January 1905. But just as it was beginning to be assumed that there would be further extensions of the lease, the message came through that demolition of the building was to start immediately.[9]

Thus the last services were held in the magnificent St James's Hall, reputedly the best concert hall in Britain, on Sunday, 12 February 1905, when the sounds of the Hallelujah Chorus rang out in Piccadilly. In the extreme emergency which followed the loss of premises used for over seventeen years, Mr Hooper of the YMCA, proprietors of the Exeter Hall, Strand (on the site of the present Strand Palace Hotel), came to the rescue and offered the use of the Hall for Sunday evening services. The members of the Mission resolved to leave the St James's Hall with heads held high. At 5.30 p.m. on the evening of Sunday 19 February over 1,500 people assembled in the corridors of the old hall and, led by the Norwood Prize Band, and with banners aloft, marched in procession to the Exeter Hall, which was crowded before the evening service began at 6.30.[10]

For a few weeks morning services were held in Hengler's Circus and evening services in Exeter Hall. But neither venue was regarded as entirely suitable. The 'atmosphere' of the circus was felt to be inappropriate to divine worship, and the Hall was considered to be too far away from the streets of the West End. Residents of Soho, it was said, rarely joined in any activities nearer the City than Charing Cross. So when the proprietors of the circus agreed to refund £100 of the annual rent it was agreed to terminate the contract with them on 18 June 1906. Then, following the Methodist Conference decision that July to allow the Mission the use of the Great Queen Street Chapel and the adjoining premises, all services were transferred there from the Exeter Hall on 7 October 1906.[11]

For the last year of his superintendency, until September 1907, Ensor Walters did not have to worry about finding a home for the Mission. Changes were made in the layout of the Great Queen Street Chapel. Pews were removed and new tip-up seats installed; the platform was moved right back against the south wall to make more room for the worshippers and an illuminated sign was placed outside the Chapel. The executive committee found the Methodist Conference plan for the redevelopment of the premises 'totally inadequate to do justice to the site and the work of the Mission', but at least, they thought, there would no longer be a need for frequent changes in the venue of the Mission.[12]

– III –

The Methodist ministry was in the family tradition of J. Ernest Rattenbury, Walters' successor as Superintendent. His grandfather, father and brother were all ministers. He was born at Stanningley, Leeds, on 10 December 1870, received his theological training at Didsbury College, Manchester, and read for his PhD at Cambridge. In the five years before he came to London in September 1907 he was Superintendent of the Nottingham circuit where he was instrumental in forming a syndicate of Methodists which purchased the Albert Hall, the largest public hall in the city. Starting with a small congregation and a £12,000 debt, he transformed the situation to establish the Mission as a centre of great social and religious activity. It was this achievement which made him a clear favourite for the Superintendency of the West London Mission.[13]

From the time in his late teens when he experienced a severe attack of scarlet fever, Ernest Rattenbury never enjoyed robust health. He was also of somewhat diminutive stature. These physical disabilities, however, only served to emphasize his great intellectual and spiritual gifts. A member of the Hinde Street congregation has a vivid recollection of her embarrassment at seeing him, in his eighties, climb with great difficulty the steps leading to the pulpit of that church. This embarrassment, however, completely disappeared, to be supplanted by wonder and admiration at his gifts of exposition and the power of his message as soon as he started to preach.[14] His scholarship was reflected in his appointment as Quillian Lecturer at Emory University, USA. On the other hand it was his ability to convey profound thoughts in the simplest language which swelled the numbers of his congregations. He maintained and enlarged the Mission's tradition of radical, applied theology so vigorously established by Hugh Price Hughes.

In 1906 for the first time a substantial number of Labour candidates were elected to Parliament. In most of the popular daily newspapers these representatives were dubbed as atheists and trouble makers. Rattenbury strongly resented these attacks which he regarded as wholly unwarranted, and he replied to them by delivering six sermons on social subjects. These appeared in book form in 1908. In the preface he wrote that the sermons were published 'as an answer to the unworthy attacks of the Press on Socialism as atheistic and immoral and also in answer to such people as suppose that advanced social views are inconsistent with an evangelical view of the gospel'. In a sermon on the Book of Revelation, Chapter 21, where St John has a vision of the Holy City, he declared:

> It is a vision of a city which is one of great wealth. Nobody has any private property in the city at all. The whole community enjoy the whole wealth of the city . . . It is a city that is evidently meant for all the nations of the world.[15]

At the same time he was wise enough to emphasize that: 'In this gospel it is always understood that men can spoil the conditions as well as conditions spoil the men.' 'Some people would turn heaven into hell in a fortnight if they got there,' he declared.

Rattenbury had been Superintendent of the Mission for only seven months when the London County Council surveyor declared that the Great Queen Street chapel, which the Trustees had renamed Kingsway Hall in April 1907, was unsafe for occupation. The executive committee which received this disturbing news on 17 April 1908 resolved as follows:

> The Executive Committee of the West London Mission having learnt that experts have pronounced that the Kingsway Hall is unsafe, is of unanimous opinion that the time has arrived to demolish the structure and erect a suitable hall and institutional premises on the site.[16]

The LCC surveyor was proved to be no scaremonger. On 7 November 1910 several workmen engaged in the demolition of the

Great Queen Street chapel were injured by a falling beam which was found to be 'quite rotten'.[17]

The consolation of knowing that the church had been warned in time did not solve the problem of finding, at very short notice, a suitable place for the congregation to worship. While the search for a more permanent home was pursued, temporary refuge was found in the new St James's Hall, Great Portland Street, from 26 March 1908. The executive committee considered the leasing of either the Coliseum or the Lyceum Theatre, with the former being regarded as 'the best bet'. However, in July, when the Coliseum directors wrote 'that it would not be in their best interests to let the building', negotiations were pressed ahead with Popular Playhouses, the proprietors of the Lyceum Theatre. In September an agreement was signed allowing the Mission the use of the theatre for morning and evening services at £25 per Sunday with £5 additional charged if the premises were required on Sunday afternoons. To ensure an impressive and memorable start to the services on Sunday 4 October 1908, large advertisement boards were displayed at the entrances to the theatre, printed cards were delivered to hotels, boarding houses and commercial premises, and a sandwich man was hired to walk up and down Kingsway and The Strand. Within the theatre, seats were reserved for nurses, policemen, and soldiers as had been the practice at St James's Hall.[18]

It was not long before the theatre was filled for the Sunday evening services. Some of those who arrived only a few minutes before the service was due to start at 7.00 p.m. found notices such as: 'Stalls, Full; Dress Circle, Full; Pit and Gallery only'. One visitor to London, seeing people flocking into the theatre, thought he would like to see the play that must be staged there, so he asked one of the church stewards whether there were any seats available. The steward said he thought that there were none left except, possibly, in one of the boxes. If the visitor cared to follow him he would go and find out. After a free seat in a box had been found, the visitor slipped a sixpence into the steward's hand and asked for a copy of the programme. On leaving the building after the service the visitor spoke to the steward (who was none other than Mr E. P. Bainbridge, the Mission's treasurer), saying that he had been 'fairly taken in', thinking he was at the Coliseum. Then he wanted to know 'who that fellow was that preached?'. On being told that it was Dr J. E. Rattenbury he replied, 'I shall come and hear him again'.[19]

Another, more distinguished, person who *did* know where he was going when he entered the theatre one Sunday evening, was the novelist, Hall Caine, who wrote of the Rattenbury sermon he heard:

> It held the people from the first word to the last. I was watching them closely. I was quite exhausted when he had finished, my sympathy and imagination were so roused. And I say that a man who preaches once like that every week has done a good week's work.[20]

Meanwhile arrangements went ahead for the preparation of a more permanent home for the Mission. On 27 July 1910 there was an unusual ceremony at Wild Court, off Kingsway. Churchgoers were familiar with stonelaying and dedication services to mark the *start* of the building of a new church. This ceremony, however, was held to launch the *demolition* of the Great Queen Street Chapel. After the Revd J. E. Rattenbury had pulled a rope which began the work of destruction there was a presentation to him from Sir Percy Bunting and the other stewards. It was of a cabinet divided into two sections, the first of which was for manuscript notes of sermons which Bunting said nobody but the preacher would be able to decipher; the second was for the typescript versions which would be easily read and a blessing to posterity.

The start of demolition was the occasion for celebration because it was the preliminary to the work of constructing the Mission's first 'permanent' home. During the preceding six years the venue of the main Sunday services had to be changed no less than five times, while the weekday activities were scattered in ten different hired buildings.

To give access to the new Kingsway Hall from the recently built (1905) thoroughfare of Kingsway a plot of land, not yet developed, was leased from the London County Council at a rent of £1,000 a year. This was an expense which was recovered from letting the International Buildings, erected at a cost of £38,000 and located either side of the Kingsway Hall entrance.[21] It was estimated that this capital outlay would be recovered in the space of thirty years. The other two parts of the new development were Wesley House, where the Mission's offices would be located, and the Institute – a new venture in the work of the church – which would be housed on the first floor, and Kingsway Hall for the conduct of the services.

6. Katherine Price Hughes, 1891

7. West London Mission
    dispensary with
    Sister Jeanette, 1889

8.   Open air congregation, 1899

9.   The crèche at Craven Hall, 1903

10. Sister Lily, 1892

11. Katherine Price Hughes
with children
in the park, 1890

12. The Sisters of the People, 1891

13. The Sisters of the People, early 1900s

Entrance to Kingsway Hall

The cost of the development, apart from the construction of International Buildings, was £71,000, including £12,000 for the acquisitions of additional land, a debt of £4,000 inherited from the Great Queen Street Chapel, and £1,500 for a new organ. As contributions towards the meeting of these outlays, £15,000 came from Methodist connexional funds, £2,000 from the late Mr Aston, £1,000 from the late Mr John Cory the coal merchant, and £1,000 each from Sir Robert Perks, William Walker and T. R. Ferens MP. Mr Andrew Carnegie, the American steel millionaire, contributed £750 to the cost of an organ, provided that an equal amount was contributed from others, and Sir Jesse Boot gave £500 for a billiard table and other equipment for the use of the Institute.[22] The balance of the cost had to be met from stonelaying gifts, class collections and appeals to the general public. When the work was completed the debt was not entirely liquidated and the bank overdraft stood at over £4,000 in December 1912.[23]

Wesley House and the Institute were officially opened a year before Kingsway Hall. On Wednesday 6 December 1911 the commemorative service to mark the opening of the offices and the Institute was conducted in the new lecture hall by the Revd C. Silvester Horne, who preached from the text: 'Praise waiteth for Thee, O God, in Zion' (Psalm 65.1). The guest speaker at the afternoon reception was to have been the Rt Hon. Walter Runciman, President of the Board of Trade. Unfortunately 'Parliamentary business' or, as it was whispered, the suffragette menace, kept him at Westminster. His place was taken by Violet Asquith, the oldest daughter of the Prime Minister.[24]

The opening of Wesley House enabled more of the work of the Mission to be concentrated under one roof. Lincoln House was closed in September 1911 and the office work, poor man's lawyer service (recently re-started), crèche and numerous classes were transferred to the new Kingsway site.[25]

Kingsway Hall, which was designed by the architect Josiah Gunton, was modelled on the great hall at West Ham.[26] It was claimed that it would hold 3,000 people, but this was only possible when extra seats were placed in some of the aisles.[27] The tip-up seats were upholstered with red velvet 'since it was hoped that it would be possible to let the hall for concerts'.[28] Acoustically it was one of the finest halls in Britain, an asset which arose from the fact that the horseshoe-shaped balcony was only seventeen metres wide and thus gave back to an orchestra an early reflection of the sounds made. Legend has it that Sir Thomas Beecham was the first to identify it as particularly well suited for recording orchestral music.[29] Until the end of the 1970s the London Symphony Orchestra used the hall regularly for its recordings.

The opening ceremony of Kingsway Hall was held on Friday 6 December 1912. It was an impressive occasion. The Lord Mayor of London, with the Sheriffs, Sword Bearer and Mace Bearer, in full regalia, sat on the front row of the platform and were accompanied by the Mayor of Holborn. The packed meeting was chaired by Gerald France MP. Josiah Gunton presented the Lord Mayor with a golden key, but it is not clear how many of the numerous doors to the hall could be opened by it or whether His Worship ever tried to open them. Since the Sir Percy Bunting memorial organ had not yet been installed, the accompaniment to the opening hymn 'All people that on earth do dwell' and following hymns was given on the piano. After the civic dignitaries had left, the President of the

Methodist Conference, the Revd Luke Wiseman, delivered a sermon from the text: 'For I have much people in this city' (Acts 18.10), in which he stressed the wonderful opportunities which opened up now that the Mission had a fine base facing one of London's main thoroughfares. After tea, served in the Lecture Hall, a much larger congregation assembled for the evening's proceedings. Once again Sir Walter Runciman sent his regrets at being unable to preside; but the cheque for £500 which he sent was found acceptable. The main address was once more delivered by the President, who pointed out that there were no traditions to hamper the work of the Mission but many to inspire it. Brief speeches of congratulation and welcome were given by the Revd Thomas Phillips of the Bloomsbury Central Baptist Church; the Revd J. L. Evans, the vicar of Holy Trinity Church, Kingsway; the Revd W. Charter-Piggott, a colleague of Sylvester Horne of the Whitefield Memorial Church in Tottenham Court Road; Dr Campbell Morgan, the well-known Congregationalist leader; the Revd J. E. Wakerley, a veteran of London Methodism; and Gipsy Smith, the evangelist. That concluded the proceedings of a very memorable day.

So many people came to the Sunday evening service two days later that an overflow service was arranged in the Lecture Hall. The Revd J. E. Rattenbury, addressing the main assembly, said that he would like the new centre to be known as 'The Father's House on Kingsway'. He stressed that all men and women were children of God and that he hoped all sorts and conditions of men and women might find joy and peace there.[30]

– IV –

In view of the many changes in venue of the main Sunday services over the years 1905–12 it is remarkable how well church membership figures were maintained. At the end of the year in which Hugh Price Hughes died (1902) the records show 1,294 full members with 213 'on trial'. These figures include those who were members in the branches at Cleveland Hall and Chalton Street and those who belonged to the Hyde Park Society. The Cleveland Hall and Chalton Street membership each fluctuated between 100 and 150, while the 'Hydeparkers' never exceeded sixty. At the time of the opening of Kingsway Hall in December 1912 there were 1,115 full members and 220 on trial, a decline of under fourteen per cent.[31]

Contributing to the buoyancy of the church membership, despite many adverse circumstances, was the successful organization of the Class system. The September 1910 issue of *Advance* lists thirty-five classes held in seven different locations. Fourteen of the classes were led by the Sisters. Some of these classes were large. The Financial Statement included in the Mission's annual report for 1909–10 shows that twenty-one members of Sister Gertrude's Tuesday class and twenty-seven members of her Wednesday class had made contributions to the Lyceum Theatre Fund.[32]

There was no letting up on the numerous social work activities of the Mission. There were separate men's and women's slate clubs at both Great Queen Street and the Chalton Hall; a servants' registry, a poor man's lawyer service and the crèche were based at Lincoln House in Greek Street; Cleveland Hall was the home of both boys' and girls' clubs and Boy Scout and Girls Life Brigade groups. There was a Men's Labour Yard in Cleveland Street, a Home of Peace for the Dying at 14 Pembridge Square, a Cheap Goods Depot at 52 Cleveland Street and a Rescue Home for young Women at 23 Ampthill Square. District visiting and health visiting – by those medically qualified – was carried out extensively by the Sisters. A number of these activities were not self-supporting. In December 1911 Mr E. P. Bainbridge, the Treasurer, informed the executive committee that over the previous five years a debt of £2,000 had been incurred in respect of the work at Cleveland Hall. Closure and transference of the work elsewhere seemed to him a serious option. This proposal was resisted by other members of the committee, and when it was pointed out that 'this was the chief section of the Mission where work for the very poor was done', Dr Rattenbury said that 'he could not take the responsibility of recommending that the Mission should turn its back on a district where it was so very much needed'.[33] By a combination of economical adminstration and successful sales of work, Sister Hope managed to keep the crèche solvent. She told her committee in February 1909 that 'the application for pieces at Frascati's Restaurant had met with success'. It was an arrangement which continued through into the war years. In December 1916 the Secretary of the Crèche Committee wrote to the restaurant's manager to thank him for 'the generous allowance of scrap' which was still being sent as a contribution to the crèche infants' dinners and Sister Hope sent the chef a Christmas card 'as from the Crèche'.[34]

There were also new ventures. During the winter of 1911–12 a PSA (Pleasant Sunday Afternoon) group was started at Wesley House. Its success encouraged Dr Rattenbury to establish the Kingsway Fellowship, with the motto 'Fellowship is Heaven and Lack of Fellowship is Hell', taken from the writings of William Morris. He told its first meeting on the afternoon of Sunday 29 September 1912 that one of the greatest weaknesses of the church in the past had been 'the exclusion of women from offices of importance'. Both men and women would be equally welcome to the Fellowship, which would be open to people of all religious or political persuasion, or none.[35] The Kingsway Fellowship, which merged with the PSA soon after its foundation, could be seen as following the tradition of Hugh Price Hughes's Sunday afternoon 'Conferences' except that Hughes's meetings were largely a vehicle for him to express his own thoughts on current issues, whereas the Fellowship was addressed by a wide variety of speakers on as great a variety of topics, religious, economic, social and political.

At the Quarterly Meeting of the Mission held on 30 June 1914 Dr Rattenbury issued a warning and a challenge. He said that he shared the members' sense of satisfaction that a 'permanent' home for the Mission was established once Kingsway Hall had been opened. 'Now there was a sense in which everyone could sit down under his own vine or fig tree,' he said. The big question was: 'Were they going to settle down to a comfortable policy combining a certain amount of religious teaching and enjoyment, or were they going to fight to make London the City of God?' If the second option was chosen, then,

> We ought to find means of reaching spiritually all the different types and classes of people in the neighbourhood, the slums, the shop assistants, the teachers, the servants – every class and condition – we must find means of studying the social conditions of life and all the various problems of social morality, and to set ourselves to find out what is needed to better the conditions of life around us.

The minutes of the meeting record that 'the leaders and stewards present felt the force of the appeal . . . and all present pledged themselves to help'.[36]

Within just over one month, alas, Britain was at war with Germany. The memories of the commitments made at the midsummer Quarterly Meeting quickly receded as the necessities of the ever-widening conflict brought other issues to the forefront of attention.

8

The Mission in World War I

It so happened that a meeting of the Mission's executive committee had been called for Tuesday 4 August 1914, the day Great Britain declared war on Germany. The war clouds had been gathering throughout the previous weekend. A state of alarm prevailed in the City. The bank rate, which had stood at four per cent on Thursday 30 July, was doubled to eight per cent the following day, and then raised again to ten per cent a day later still. This was particularly bad news for the Mission, which had a bank overdraft in excess of £4,000 at the time. Dr Rattenbury told the Committee that the prospects were of a sharp fall in revenue from lettings of Kingsway Hall and of a sharp rise in the cost of maintaining the overdraft. Drastic economies would have to be made. The committee therefore decided to dismiss all the employees at Kingsway Hall, with the exception of Mr and Mrs Smart, the caretakers; to dispense with the quartet employed for the Sunday services; to dismiss all but two of the office staff; to cancel all advertisements and to suspend publication of *Advance*. Even more draconian was the decision to close Cleveland Hall, the People's Hall, Chalton Street, the crèche, the old clothes depot, the rescue home and Katherine House (the home of many of the Sisters). A few Sisters were to be accommodated in Kingsway Hall where most of the members' classes would be held. Finally it was decided to invite Mission members to undertake the cleaning of the hall and other rooms.[1]

When the committee met again six days later calmer counsels prevailed. Dr Rattenbury reported that he had received a deputation of the People's Hall, Chalton Street, workers who had offered to continue the Sunday work at their own expense. This offer was gratefully accepted. Sister Hope had opposed most strongly the

73

proposal to close the crèche and was supported by Mr Hayman, a member of the crèche committee, who had offered to guarantee its financial position. Hence this valuable service to working mothers and their babies continued throughout the war years. It was also decided not to close the old clothes depot and to continue, after all, the advertisements of services and meetings. The knowledge that the bank rate had been brought down to six per cent four days before no doubt encouraged a more relaxed attitude at this second wartime meeting.[2]

Nevertheless, Cleveland Hall and Katherine House were relinquished as planned: the former was leased to a firm of flag makers while, through the intervention of Mrs Gordon McArthur, the latter was converted into a 'Hostel for Poor Ladies'. The suspension of the work at Cleveland Hall led to the resignation of the four Sisters who had worked there, so that by the end of 1914 the greater part of the Sisterhood was accommodated at Kingsway Hall. Through these and other economy measures the bank overdraft was reduced to £2,732 after only five months of war.[3] The generous offers of accommodation from the Revd Walter Pigot of Whitefields and the Revd H. G. Roberts of Hinde Street Methodist Church enabled some of the activities, including mothers' meetings, Sunday schools, boys' clubs, girls' clubs and a young people's society, formerly conducted at Cleveland Hall and the People's Hall, Somers Town, to be continued.

– II –

On Sunday, 2 August 1914, prominent leaders of the Labour Party, including H. M. Hyndman, Keir Hardie and Arthur Henderson, addressed a big meeting in Trafalgar Square protesting against the drift to war. Again, while the executive committee of the Mission was deliberating in Wesley House on that fateful fourth of August, a large meeting in Kingsway Hall of the National Union of Women's Suffrage Societies was listening to Mrs Henry Fawcett denouncing war mobilization in Europe and demanding British neutrality.[4]

The venerable Dr John Clifford, former President of the National Free Church Council, who had led pacifist opposition to the Boer War, also declared in favour of 'a rigorous abstention from joining in the war'.[5] The news of the German invasion of Belgium on 4 August changed the balance of opinion with remarkable rapidity.

Three days after she had delivered her Kingsway Hall speech Mrs Fawcett declared herself wholeheartedly behind the war effort: 'Now is the time for resolute effort and self-sacrifice on the part of every one of us to help our country,' she urged.[6]

Dr Clifford's conversion to the war party was equally rapid (though he did speak out boldly, later on, in defence of the rights of conscientious objectors). Since Germany had 'trampled under foot with ineffable scorn the rights of small nationalities,' he said, 'it was as just as it was necesary, not only in the interests of little Belgium, but for the security and autonomy of small states all over the world, that Britain should take her stand in an entirely unselfish service for the good of mankind.'[7]

Most of the earnest young men who attended the Kingsway Fellowship meetings on Sunday afternoons to work out a Christian attitude to current social and political questions were stirred by appeals such as those made by Dr Clifford. They flocked in large numbers to volunteer for the armed forces. It is impossible to say how many joined that 'unreturning army that was youth',[8] but in September 1915 *Advance* (which had resumed publication the previous December) noted that 'twenty per cent of the regular congregations' of August 1914 was 'then in one or other of the services'.[9] A year later the editor wrote, 'It is difficult to say how many men with some connection or other with the Mission are in the fighting line, but there are many hundreds of them.'[10] Dr Rattenbury printed letters received from soldiers at the front. A 'Conscientious Fighter' wrote from 'Somewhere in France' on 26 June 1916 to congratulate the Superintendent on a sermon, preached at Kingsway Hall and reported in *The British Weekly*. When Dr Rattenbury said that 'there was a danger in our people coming to the conclusion that the conscientious objector was the only man who had acted from conscientious motives' the congregation applauded.[11] However, Rifleman W. B. Chenery seemed less certain that the issue was so simple. From his trench he wrote:

> I have often wondered, whilst watching those long lines of German trenches, as the grey dawn steals into the sky, and the cold nips hands and feet, whether one could really hate another who is more or less undergoing the same experience as oneself. Furthermore, I have never heard a comrade say that he hates the enemy in the true sense of the word.[12]

The heroism and tragedy incidental to the war on the Western Front are manifested in some of the reports. Private Sweet, a member of the Mission church, died rescuing the wounded captain of his Company, Captain Ward Hunt. 'Private Sweet got him on his back. As he was carrying him back, one of the enemy machine guns cut them down, killing both instantly.'[13] By the autumn of 1916 *Advance* reported that there were ninety-two names on the Institute Roll of Honour and Dr Rattenbury proposed that a small chapel should be formed at Kingsway by making it from a room just outside the Lecture Hall. On 13 November 1916 this was dedicated to 'the Glory of God and the memory of the men who have given their lives for King and Country'.[14]

One result of the Mission church being denuded of 'the large majority of its male members' was a shortage of Sunday School teachers. In the summer of 1915 no less than eight of the classes were looking for new leaders.[15] More permanently, the balance between men and women in the congregation was altered, reflecting the fact that nationally the number of women over fourteen years of age in the population rose from 595 per 1,000 persons in 1911 to 638 per 1,000 in 1921.[16]

– III –

The destruction of life and property caused by air raids on London between 1914 and 1918 was very small compared with the devastation of the Second World War. The fifty-two Zeppelin raids between January 1915 and August 1918 killed 495 persons and injured 1,236. The fifty-nine aeroplane raids over the same span of time killed 618 and injured 1,650.[17] One Mission activity which was affected by the outbreak of war was the holding of open air magic lantern services, which were 'discontinued in September 1914 owing to the new regulation about lights'.[18] Following Zeppelin raids on London on 12 and 13 October 1915 receipts from the Saturday evening concerts fell from £26 to £10 and it was therefore decided to discontinue the concerts during the winter months.[19] Compared with the air raid precautions enforced from 3 September 1939, the precautions taken in the First World War were spasmodic and amateurish. No complete blackout was enforced until the summer of 1916.[20] It was the custom of the War Office to send private warnings of raids to police stations, newspaper offices, hospitals, fire brigade stations and government departments, but decisions on how to notify the general public varied from locality to locality. In London police cars drove through the streets displaying 'Take Cover' notices on their windscreens or policemen were sent out on bicycles blowing whistles.[21] It was not until 11 June 1915, when some fire extinguishers were ordered, that any action was taken by the Mission to deal with the possibility of air raids. In the autumn of 1917, however, raids by both aeroplanes and Zeppelins were intensified. On 13 October bombs fell in nearby Wellington Street in front of the Lyceum Theatre, where the play *The Scarlet Pimpernel* was being produced. By the spring of 1918 the editor of *Advance* was writing of 'the widespread unsettlement and repeated interruptions of the raids causing a most painful strain of body and mind'. The severe raids of October 1917 caused a decline in the number of children attending the crèche, despite the fact that Sister Hope had made arrangements for relays of them to be sent to Pevensey on the Sussex coast where they could have the benefit of fresh air and freedom from the strain of the raids.[22] By this time Londoners had got into the habit of resorting to the underground stations when there was warning of an air raid, though this was not done on a regular, nightly, basis as was the case in the Second World War.

– IV –

It has often been pointed out that the war opened up new employment opportunities for women. This was undoubtedly true in the longer run. For some months after August 1914, however, the war had an adverse effect on the employment of women in the West London area. The peace time 'rag trade' had provided women with a great deal of 'home work', even though it was irregularly provided and very poorly paid. One result of the war fever that swept the country in the autumn of 1914 was that in a wave of patriotic feeling, middle- and upper-class women turned their minds from dress and millinery to higher things, and in so doing threw more than forty per cent of their labouring sisters out of work or on short time.[23] In a further demonstration of patriotism many of those who had formerly employed domestic servants determined to dispense with one or more of their maids. Over the country as a whole the number of women employed in domestic service fell from

1,658,000 in 1914 to 1,258,000 in 1918.[24] The Sisters of the People found that there was a new emphasis to their work. They gave temporary work to those women who had lost their jobs and to those whose husbands had rushed to enlist and who were experiencing delays in the receipt of their dependents' allowances.

However, it was not long before new job opportunities opened up for women. Even before the outbreak of war the number of female telegraphists employed by the Post Office was increasing rapidly, but the quick surge of enlistment of men from the big London offices brought a vast acceleration of women's employment. By 1918 'the male clerk with his quill pen and copperplate handwriting had gone for good. The female shorthand typist took his place.'[25] At railway stations, on board trains, or in railway sidings, women were to be seen issuing and collecting tickets, moving passengers' luggage, or cleaning carriages. Over 30,000 of them took the place of enlisted men between 1914 and 1918. But the most persistent call was for 'Molly the munitions worker'. By November 1918 there were 947,000 of them. Their working life was arduous and monotonous. Generally they worked a ten-hour day with two hours allowed for meal breaks. But in times when there were shell shortages their working day was extended to twelve hours, for ten of which they would be standing, operating a noisy machine in a humid atmosphere.[26]

As they performed effectively more and more jobs which had hitherto been regarded as suitable only for men, the self-assurance of women was increased. The paternalism of the owners of the big London department stores declined as rapidly rising food prices in the early months of the war persuaded them to end their shop assistants 'living in' on the premises. This made it more difficult for the women to make ends meet, since they had to find their own accommodation, but at the same time it increased their self-reliance.

In peacetime one of the biggest causes of broken marriages and the resort to prostitution was the drunkenness of the husband. After an Order in Council was passed on 10 June 1915 prohibiting the opening of public houses before noon and in the afternoon from 2.30 convictions for drunkenness fell sharply. They averaged 3,388 per week in 1914, but only 449 a week in 1918.[27] But as the slaughter on the war fronts continued, new social problems took the place of the old. Dr Rattenbury was keenly aware of the changes that were taking place when he wrote:

> The increased disproportion of the sexes will make marriage impossible for many women. Through this terrible war there will be many a widowed maid who will have to change her hopes of a happy married life because the loved one will never come back.[28]

In the harsh conditions of war old standards of morality were increasingly challenged:

> Life was less than cheap: it was thrown away. The religious teaching that the body was the temple of the Holy Ghost could mean little or nothing to those who saw it mutilated and destroyed in millions by Christian nations engaged in war . . . Little wonder that the old ideals of chastity and self control in sex were, for many, also lost.[29]

Whereas in peacetime it was the desperate need to feed hungry children that often drove women to prostitution, in the war it was,

> The grey and sordid monotony of the badly paid girl engaged in some unskilled, uninteresting work just at that age when romance and adventure and the first stirrings of sexual feeling make her demand from life, colour and beauty and interest and love, that was the real cause of the mischief.[30]

Dr Rattenbury saw clearly that a prime responsibility of the Mission was to offer a sense of Christian direction and purpose to those who were adrift and bewildered in the maelstrom of war. His evening services, in particular, met a real need. Attendances in March 1915 reached their maximum since Kingsway Hall opened and in the following month they were reported as 'never more crowded'.[31] In the darkest days of the war the Superintendent kept shining a beacon of hope for the future. Speaking in June 1917 to the text 'Preach the Gospel' (Mark 16.15), he declared:

> And if the Gospel is ever brought home, the gospel of God's grace working both in the individual and social order, if it ever be brought home, it must be emphasised from both points of view. It must have this social as well as the individual application.[32]

Dr Rattenbury was a more thoughtful and widely read person than was the Mission's founder. He lacked Hugh Price Hughes's impetuous 'black and white' certainty on what was right and what was wrong. Although he considered that the support for small nations against the aggression of their powerful neighbours was a just cause, he also saw the incompatibility of the practices of war with the teachings of the Christian gospel. This distress of mind brought its physical consequences. He was away from his post, ill, from October 1917 to September 1918.

In July 1917, not long before the onset of Dr Rattenbury's illness, the Methodist Conference decided that the Methodist Churches at Hinde Street and Warwick Gardens should join the West London Mission circuit. This important new partnership began in September 1917 in the absence of the guiding hand of the Mission's Superintendent.

9

Hinde Street

– I –

There is no doubt that the reason for including the Warwick Gardens, Kensington, chapel in the West London Mission circuit in 1917 was that attendances there had declined sharply during the early years of the war. The chapel, which had been opened in 1863, drew large congregations during the outstanding ministry of Dr Morley Punshon between 1873–5, but these were largely made up of the preacher's own devotees who came from all parts of London and further afield, and they disappeared with his departure. The membership from the immediate neighbourhood was always small.[1] Under the terms of the agreement reached in 1917 the executive committee of the Mission accepted the inclusion of the Warwick Gardens community for an experimental period of five years, only provided that Kingsway was not involved in any additional expense as a result of the arrangement. In the event the link was maintained until 1925, when the resolution of the executive committee of 4 April 1924 that it wished to be relieved of responsibility in the matter came into effect.[2]

Hinde Street was a very different case. Writing in the Mission's magazine, Dr Rattenbury admitted that Hinde Street had 'quite as much to give, perhaps more than to receive, by combination' with the West London Mission.[3] Membership was well sustained during the war; the small decline from 323 in 1913 to 283 in 1917 was very creditable in the light of the fact that conscription was operating. The decline in numbers at Kingsway was greater.

– II –

When writing that Hinde Street had 'much to give' Dr Rattenbury was no doubt recalling the remarkable contribution to Christian

HINDE STREET METHODIST CHAPEL

Origins and Connections

John Wesley's London Societies

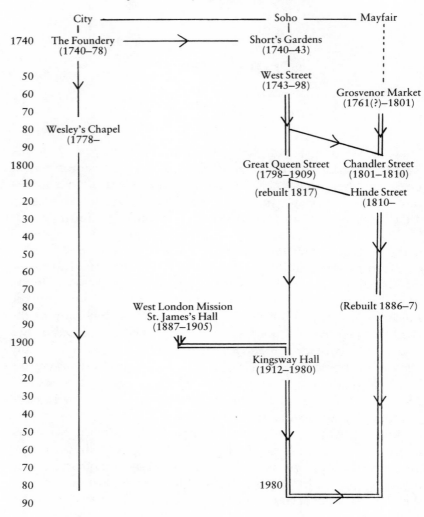

City	Soho	Mayfair
1740 The Foundery (1740–78)	Short's Gardens (1740–43)	
50	West Street (1743–98)	
60		Grosvenor Market (1761(?)–1801)
70		
80 Wesley's Chapel (1778–		
90		
1800	Great Queen Street (1798–1909)	Chandler Street (1801–1810)
10	(rebuilt 1817)	Hinde Street (1810–
20		
30		
40		
50		
60		
70		
80 West London Mission St. James's Hall (1887–1905)		(Rebuilt 1886–7)
90		
1900		
10	Kingsway Hall (1912–1980)	
20		
30		
40		
50		
60		
70		
80	1980	
90		

Movements of parts of a Society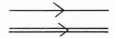

Movements of Societies

82

witness over more than a century given by members of that West End church and remembering the unique links which some of its founders had with the Wesley brothers.

Figure 1 shows the antecedents of the Hinde Street Church. Particularly important are its immediately antecedent links with the West Street, Grosvenor Market and Chandler Street chapels, since leaders who were active in the life of these earlier church communities played a significant part in the foundation of the Hinde Street Church in 1810.

Hinde Street Chapel

The most important early centre of Methodist worship in West London was the chapel in West Street near Cambridge Circus which was built for a community of Huguenot refugees and opened in 1700. By 1743 the chapel had passed into the hands of the Methodists and John Wesley had delivered the first of many sermons he preached there. Based on the westward movement of population and trade from the old City of London area the number of Methodists increased rapidly. When the lease of the West Street Chapel and Chapel House expired in 1798 some members of the congregation joined another community of Methodists who had for many years been worshipping in a room above a slaughter house in Grosvenor Market near Grosvenor Square and near to the westernmost limits of London's eighteenth-century development. The main society moved into a chapel in Great Queen Street near present-day Kingsway.[4]

It was not long before the congregation at Grosvenor Market was too large for the limited accommodation available, so that in 1801 a chapel was opened in Chandler Street (subsequently renamed Robert Street and, later still, Weighhouse Street), a short street running parallel to Oxford Street on its south side. By 1807, when the West London circuit was formed, it was already recognized that the Chandler Street chapel was too small for the needs of the rapidly growing membership. It is at this point that the link between the Wesleys and Hinde Street chapel becomes manifest. The Superintendent of the new circuit was the Revd Henry Moore, who was ordained by John Wesley and from 1785 until Wesley's death six years later served as his assistant, each weekday at 5.00 a.m. reading out the letters received by the latest post and helping to compose the replies.[5] Moore presided over the first Quarterly Meeting of the West London circuit held on 1 October 1807 when the question of building a new chapel for the Chandler Street membership was considered. The fifteenth resolution declared that:

> a new chapel at the West End of the town was greatly wanted, instead of Chandler Street which was evidently too small, and that ground should be taken or purchased for the same.

The sixteenth resolution stated that 'ground might be had at the corner of Thayer Street near Manchester Square' and appointed a committee to proceed with the arrangements for its purchase.

More than sixty years earlier Jacob Hinde, who was lessee of nine twenty-fourths of the Marylebone Park estate, had married Anne Thayer, and before he died in 1802 he had given her maiden name to one of the streets that bounded the property, and his own surname to the other.

The trustees, who had been nominated by Henry Moore, encountered prolonged and frustrating legal difficulties in acquiring the site. Even when it was believed that the transaction had been completed and the documents had been signed by the vendor and purchaser, more obstacles arose. The Duke of Portland and his steward wanted the land for building a National School (a Church of England denominational school) and they seized upon the fact that the agreement for the transfer of the land had been signed on a piece of unstamped paper to declare that the transaction was invalid and that the Methodist trustees should surrender their claim to the property.[6]

What was described by a later Hinde Street minister as 'the most important meeting ever held at Chandler Street Chapel' considered how to reply to the Duke of Portland's demand. At first a majority of those present were in favour of a policy of surrender, some out of deference to the Duke, some on the grounds that, as a religious body, they should favour policies of peace, and some arguing that the Duke's intervention was an act of Providence which it would be folly to gainsay. Henry Moore who, as Superintendent, took the chair at the meeting, would have none of this backsliding. With great firmness he told the meeting:

> I will not consent to your relinquishing the ground which God in His providence has put into your hands; we will abide the issue of the gentleman's legal threats; write to him at once and tell him so.[7]

This decisiveness settled the legal issue. The attempt by the opposition party to dispute the Methodist trustees' claim to the land was abandoned. On 30 June 1809 four tenders were received for the building of the church and the lowest, from Mr Thomas Hughes, for £5,245, was accepted.[8] This first Hinde Street Church (shown in plate 15) was designed in early Regency style by the Revd William Jenkins, one of John Wesley's itinerant preachers, who, after retirement from the ministry, devoted his remaining years to designing Methodist chapels. The building was often derisively referred to as the Dutch Oven because it was high and wide but short from front to rear. The site on which it was built had been an unsightly swamp and it was therefore considered necessary to place the building on 'stilts'. However, before construction began the trustees were warned that there might still be opposition from the Church of England party in the neighbourhood. They were advised to deposit bricks and timber on the site at the earliest possible opportunity to make good their claim to the land. So at five o'clock one morning in early July 1809 Mr Calder, one of the trustees, put the first brick on the ground. If he thought that at such an early hour the opposition party would still be abed he was mistaken. As soon as bricks and timber were brought to the site they were thrown off it by members of the parish church. Despite these setbacks, the Methodists persisted and eventually established their physical presence as they had earlier made good their legal claim.[9]

When the foundation stone of the chapel was laid on Tuesday 11 July 1809 the workmen received a present of one shilling each, about one-twentieth of their weekly wage, or approximately £5 in modern equivalent.

By the time the building was completed and the first services were held in August 1810 the cost of construction had gone up to £6,458. 8s. 10d., well above the £5,245 of Mr Hughes's estimate. The war against Napoleon was partly responsible. The Baltic ports from which building timber was normally obtained were closed to commerce in 1809 and the contractors were obliged to resort to the more expensive supplies available in Portugal and Spain. Since the greater part of the cost of construction was paid in borrowed money, the ultimate cost of the chapel, after interest on loans had been paid, was £15,000.[10] The rough equivalent in 1985 prices would be £130,000.

Membership at Hinde Street grew rapidly from 234 in 1810 to a peak of 1,127 in 1844, a figure which included 105 for old Milton Street chapel. But the burden of the heavy debt, not finally extinguished until 1878, greatly limited the scope of church activities. There was enough room in the main body of the chapel and its two galleries to seat 1,000 – not all of them in the greatest comfort. Other space, for class meetings, the Sunday School and Band of Hope, was extremely limited and many meetings took place in the class leaders' homes or makeshift accommodation in nearby buildings.[11]

Up to 1863 when a harmonium was installed, the music for congregational singing was led by a choir under the direction of a precentor, originally serving for £6 a year but with salary raised to £40 in 1844. The opening note was provided by a violinist while the bass note was given on the viol. In the mid-century years the number of instruments was increased to three violins, a bass viol, two flageolets, a clarinet, a flute and a serpent. An organ, which cost £245, but the woodwork casing of which was erected free of charge by Mr Brown, a builder of Marylebone High Street, was installed in 1864.[12]

The Victorians considered that the proper way to give due respect to those who had recently died was to apply black crêpe on a lavish scale to cover not only the funeral horses but also the pulpit from which the funeral or memorial service was conducted. Hinde Street conformed to this generally accepted practice whenever one of the ministers died while still in the service of the church.[13]

The early church community at Hinde Street was made up of a mixture of prosperous business and professional families on the one hand and artisans, labourers and domestic servants on the other. The important offices of the church, including the trustees, class leaders and Sunday School visitors (later called Superintendents) were all held by members of the more prosperous families. The first list of trustees, which includes twenty-one names, exclusively male, was headed by John Jenkins, 'Gentleman', of Edgware Road, who subscribed £100 towards the building of the chapel. Joseph Butterworth (1770–1826), listed as a 'Fleet Street Bookseller', was the founder of the famous firm of law book publishers to the crown; William Kent headed the best known firm of stationers in West London; John Clemence was a builder of Marylebone who tendered (unsuccessfully) for the work of building Hinde Street Chapel. The remainder of the trustees were all tradesmen, including two tailors, a bootmaker, a shoemaker, a cordwainer, a haberdasher, a cabinet maker, an ironmonger, a cheesemonger, a silver plater, a japanner, a chair maker, another stationer, a turner and a medicine vendor.[14] They were all men of some substance in the trading communities of West London or of Lambeth, where there was also a strong Methodist community. However, most notable of the members of the early Hinde Street church were Charles Wesley's children.

Among other distinguished persons who gave strong support to the work of the church at Hinde Street was the portrait painter John Jackson, RA (1778–1831), who served as a poor steward in 1825 and as a Circuit Steward in 1831. He exhibited 146 pictures at the Royal Academy between 1804 and 1830 and was elected Royal Academician in 1817. Many of his portraits, which were said to be executed with 'a marvellous alacrity of hand', were painted in his studio at 7 Newman Street, close to the site of the present-day Middlesex Hospital. It was there that he composed many of the illustrations which he contributed to the *Methodist Magazine*. His biographer noted that 'the low state of his finances at his death is partly attributed to his extravagant generosity in support of Wesleyan institutions'.[15] W. H. Smith (1825–1891), who in 1862 secured the exclusive right of selling books and newspapers on all the important railways in England, was, with his family, a member of the Great Queen Street Methodist Chapel, but for many years he paid the stipend of the third minister employed in the Hinde Street circuit.[16]

No other Methodist church in Britain could claim such a distinguished succession of superintendents and ministers as did Hinde Street in the nineteenth century. Seventeen men were at different times elected President of the Methodist Conference during their period of service at the chapel; a further eight ministers occupied the presidential chair at some other time during their careers.[17] During his three years in the circuit (1842–4), Robert Young, through his zeal and eloquence, attracted 800 new members. However, 1857–9 may be considered the golden years of the Methodist ministry in the chapel. The four ministers then in post included George B. Macdonald, T. Llewellyn, F. Greeves and W. M. Punshon. Of these Punshon was the favourite with the congregations. When it was known that he was preaching there would be crowds on the entrance steps of 'that grim piece of unimaginative brickwork' an hour before the start of the evening service. Macdonald, by contrast, came to be distinguished by his progeny, rather than by his eloquence. Of his seven children, one, Alice (1837–1910), was the mother of Rudyard Kipling; a second, Georgiana (1840–1920), married Sir Edward Burne Jones, the pre-Raphaelite painter; and a third, Louisa (1845–1925), was the mother of Stanley Baldwin, who was Prime Minister in 1923–4, 1924–9, and 1935–7.[18] Not all the earlier ministers had the eloquence of Robert Newton, who helped to give the work of the new chapel an excellent start between 1812–13. The Revd Thomas Stanley had a reputation for being long-winded; but he sometimes compensated for this with his quick-wittedness. A sailor who attended his service at Sheerness one evening grew impatient with the preacher's laboured delivery. From the back of the church he called out: 'Come, Sir, crowd in a little more sail there.' To which Stanley replied in a flash, 'I will, as soon as I have weathered this Point.'[19]

– III –

In surveying the activities of the Hinde Street church community over a period of more than a century before the link with the West London Mission was made in 1917, the outstanding achievement is seen to be the work of the Sunday School. This is manifest when comparison is made with the social work pioneered by the West London Mission after 1887. From the Hinde Street pulpit there rarely came outspoken denunciations of the evils of the social system such as were delivered by Hugh Price Hughes from St James's Hall or J. Ernest Rattenbury from the Lyceum Theatre. On the other hand, thousands of children were given disciplined teaching. In 1886 it was estimated that nearly 23,000 children had received training in the Hinde Street Sunday School and in the various branch schools such as those at Hampstead, Peter Street, Stanhope Street, Bayswater, and so on. Some idea of the number of scholars involved can be gained from the quantity of special Sunday School Anniversary hymn sheets ordered. The number rose from 1750 per year from 1831–6 inclusive to 2000 per year in 1842.[20] For about the first thirty years in the life of the Sunday School many of the children admitted to the classes were unable to read or write. Hence one finds ordered from Kent's the stationers, '50 alphabets on boards, 100 Spellings part 1 and 50 part II'.[21]

On the morning of 30 July 1815, out of the thirteen new scholars admitted, seven were sweeps' 'climbing boys'. The minute records:

> They appeared very clean considering their work, and very desirous of learning to read and write. They say there is nothing to hinder them attending constantly and early . . . There is one sweep in the school, who when he was admitted could not read at all, but now is in writing.[22]

The children were given a rigorous training. Their hours of attendance at Sunday School were from nine until twelve noon and from two to half-past four in the afternoon. In summer the rules stated that they were to assemble again at half-past five in the evening to be conducted in due order by the teachers to public worship.

The object sought by the teachers might be summed up in the words of the educationist the Revd Andrew Bell, who sought 'the improvement in the subordination, and orderly conduct, and general behaviour of the children'.[23] Even as late as 1873 the Methodist Conference recommended the following guide lines in its *General Rules* for Sunday schools:

> To instruct and train scholars in the doctrines, privileges and duties of the Christian religion; only so much secular teaching as is necessary to

secure this end shall be given in it on the Sabbath day. The Holy Scriptures and the Catechisms of the Wesleyan Methodists shall be used as the means of such instruction and training.[24]

On leaving the Sunday School young people were given every encouragement to join one of the many week-night devotional classes. Their teachers assembled each week in the Leaders' Meetings, which kept the welfare and conduct of each class member under close surveillance. From the minutes of these meetings we learn that on 23 August 1814 Charles Leonard was put out of membership for Sabbath-breaking by selling spruce beer. In February of the following year a member who had been required by his employer to work on the Sabbath was told that he must either relinquish his employment or give up his membership of the church. In this case, mercifully, he was able to persuade his employer to eliminate the Sunday work.[25]

However, it would be very misleading to suggest that all Hinde Street activities were characterized by a martinet-style discipline. The weekly Mothers Meeting was welcomed by many women for the temporary relief that it brought from a seemingly unending round of domestic chores. The Girls 'At Home', which also met weekly, was designed to promote the welfare of young people employed in the rapidly expanding West End businesses, and the 'Young Men's Social Gathering' gave the opportunity to the Mr Kippses of the big department stores to join in games, music, refreshments and discussions on topics of interest.[26]

The spiritual fellowship of Hinde Street members in early Victorian times was one of the great strengths of the church. N. Curnoch noted that, 'On the evening of Christmas Day 1842 a lovefeast was held at Hinde Street Chapel at which about 900 people were present. Thirty-four persons spoke with much propriety and power . . . an indescribable awe rested on the assembly.'

– IV –

By 1878, as a result of a succession of subscription teas, bazaars and special appeals launched over a long period of years, the Hinde Street chapel was at last free of debt. At the same time membership figures were buoyant around the 375–400 level in the late 1870s and early 1880s. At the circuit quarterly meeting in April 1883, therefore, it was proposed by Mr W. T. Eastman, seconded by Mr W. Johnson and carried:

> That this meeting is of opinion that the time has now come when the Trustees should take into consideration the necessity of rebuilding Hinde Street Chapel.[27]

It was not until the closing weeks of 1885 that the building committee began to take the necessary steps to implement the resolution. Thereafter decisions were taken in rapid succession. Mr James Weir (1845–1905), designer of many chapels in the London area, was appointed architect. The new church was to be built in the Italianate style with a two-storied portico, but also incorporating a high-angled turret. On 14 May 1886 the tender for £14,350, including the sum of £3,300 for the purchase of an adjoining house, submitted by Mr James Holloway, being the lowest estimate, was accepted by the trustees. (The ultimate cost was £17,000.) The old chapel was closed on 23 May and services were transferred to the nearby Steinway Hall until July 1887, when they were resumed at 19 Thayer Street pending the opening of the new church on 29 September.[28]

The ceremony of laying the foundation stone of the new chapel was held on 4 August 1886, when the President of the Methodist Conference, the Revd R. N. Young, gave a short address in which he enjoined the younger generation of worshippers who would be occupying the new church to maintain 'the old truths, with the old ring and the old prayer'. Buried in a receptacle near the first stone was a sealed bottle containing current issues of *The Times* and *The Methodist Recorder*, a portrait of Dr Young and a parchment bearing the names of the church trustees and the architect.[29] The church was built with remarkable speed. On Saturday 7 May 1887, amid beautiful spring sunshine, the topstone of the steeple was laid by the Revd W. J. Brown, the circuit superintendent. To reach the spot – from which there was an excellent view of west London – the minister and a dozen other persons 'of agile limb and steady nerve' climbed a series of vertical ladders. After God's blessing had been invoked on the future of a great undertaking the ceremony closed with the singing of 'All Hail the Power of Jesus' Name' and the Doxology.[30]

Bishop and Son rebuilt the old 1864 organ in the new church at a cost of £178 in July 1887.[31]

At 2.30 p.m. on Thursday, 29 September 1887, the invalid Mrs Johnson, wife of the chief circuit steward, was driven to the entrance of the new church in an open Victoria and with difficulty ascended the steps to the entrance. Sir George Chubb presented her with a silver key which she used to open the centre front door. The ceremony was followed by a service conducted by the Revd J. Walton, the President of the Methodist Conference. There were special commemorative services on the three following Sundays and the celebrations ended with a tea and a public meeting on 18 October, when the Revd Drs Osborn, Rigg, Greeves and Hugh Price Hughes were among the preachers.[32]

Money had been borrowed to complete the building and furnishing of the church. In January 1888 a 'temporary loan' was made by the Star Life Assurance Company. With vivid memories still retained about the crippling effects of debt on the old chapel there was determination not to repeat the experience. A Debt Liquidation Committee was appointed in 1898, and several special teas, bazaars and appeals later it was announced on 3 July 1899 that the debt had been extinguished.[33]

As we have seen in Chapter 2, great concern was expressed by the Hinde Street Quarterly Meeting on 28 June 1886 lest the establishment of the West London Mission should result in the loss of the old established chapel's younger members. Hugh Price Hughes tried to allay these fears by claiming that the work of the new mission would strengthen West End Methodism rather than weaken it. The aim of the new venture was not to draw adherents from other churches but to win non-believers for Christ. At first it looked as if Hinde Street fears were fully justified as membership fell from 395 in 1885–6 to 221 in 1893. However, when Jane T. Stoddart conducted a religious census for the *Daily News* in 1902–3, she found that Hinde Street's membership had shot up to 701. In any case the earlier decline may have had more to do with the temporary decline in popularity of the ministers rather than to any poaching of members by the newly founded West London Mission. Great Queen Street, on the other hand, did suffer a severe drop in membership – from 922 in 1886 to 394 in 1902–3.[34]

Certainly the greater space provided in the new premises provided the opportunity for the work of the Sunday school and the Band of Hope Society to expand. The number of children in the

Sunday school books increased from 317 in 1884 to 454 in 1897, and some of the recently recruited Wesley deaconesses, notably Sisters Clare and Margery, were pressed into service as teachers.[35] The Band of Hope Society, which was established in 1877, flourished in the 1890s, when some of its open meetings were attended by more than 300 persons. Visiting speakers were welcomed. (But sometimes the comments about them in the committee minutes were far from complimentary. Of the speaker who came from Regent's Park College on 15 January it was written: 'He was a duffer'.) More than once Mr J. Burgess gave lectures on temperance 'with chemical experiments'. The society received visiting deputations from railwaymen, postmen, teetotal soldiers from the Woolwich garrison, policemen and many others.[36]

In 1917, at the time when the Hinde Street community was joined in the same circuit with the West London Mission, one of its ministers, the Revd H. Bisseker, gave a valuable description of the church congregation:

Our constituency is of a somewhat varied character. The permanent nucleus of our congregation is formed by a number of devoted families, happily drawn alike from the larger and from the less wealthy homes of the neighbourhood. The majority, however, of those who worship with us are men and women living away from home, who have been called to reside in this part of London by the requirements of their present work. Some of these are assisting in the large business houses of the West End; others are engaged in positions of domestic trust; others again are university students or nurses in London hospitals; while yet others, we rejoice to think, are girls in domestic service, who far separated from their friends of their earlier days have found a new circle of friendships within the walls of the church. Add to these girls of the WAAC and such soldiers in training and in hospital or on leave, as we are able to get in touch with, and the picture is complete.[37]

It was that 'permanent nucleus of a number of devoted families' which was keen to maintain the separate identity of the Hinde Street Church and ensured the writing into the agreement with the West London Mission at Kingsway safeguards for their continued independence. The first paragraphs of the typed statement clarifying the relationship between the two churches included the declaration that 'the union would be of a kind to maintain Hinde

Street's autonomy as a church with 107 years of Methodist history which for many reasons it is desirable to maintain'. Hinde Street was guaranteed 'complete administrative and financial independence in its own church affairs'; it had the freedom to arrange its own church work and make its own plan. The Hinde Street trust was to continue in being with power to elect its own treasurer, secretary and chapel stewards. Paragraph five of the agreement made clear the procedure for the invitations to ministers:

> All ministerial invitations shall be given by the London Committee on the nomination of the Mission circuit stewards, but in the case of Hinde Street the London Committee shall accept the nomination of the Hinde Street Church Council.

To give a greater degree of unity to the linking of the churches the final paragraph stated that 'for the purpose of consolidating the work of this enlarged West London Mission Circuit' the Mission Quarterly Meeting was 'to receive reports of the progress of the work at Hinde Street as of the other branches of work of the Mission'.[38]

Undoubtedly in 1917 the traditions of the West London Mission and the Hinde Street Church seemed to be very different. The Mission had come into being as an expression of the Forward Movement with its message that the Christian gospel was incomplete if it was not given a social and political, as well as a personal, expression. Many of the Superintendents and trustees of the Hinde Street church, on the other hand, placed far more emphasis on personal salvation, and they considered it dangerous and divisive for ministers to express forthright views on current political issues. It remained to be seen how meaningful the alliance of the two church communities would be.

10

The Inter-War Years

– I –

The First World War has been described as 'the greatest watershed in modern British history'. However, its effects were 'as much concerned with accelerating as with diverting the course of social history'.[1] Everywhere in the 1920s there was a widespread feeling that the old order had passed away. There was a marked generation gap in manners, dress and, above all, outlook, between those who were in their prime in the Edwardian era and the young adults of the 1920s and 1930s.

One change for the better in London was that there was less poverty than there had been in pre-war days. The average earnings of all workers on full time rose by 94% between 1914 and 1924. Since the cost of living over the same span of time rose by only 74%, the rise in real wages was 11%.[2] H. Llewellyn-Smith, who conducted a survey of life and labour in London in the early 1930s, found:

> The fact that the average workman in London can now buy a third more of articles of consumption in return for labour of an hour's duration per day affords conclusive proof that the material conditions under which the mass of London workers live have considerably improved.[3]

That, however, was a statement about the *average* London workman. The capital city still contained great contrasts between one borough and another and between the different social classes. In the side streets off the brightly lit thoroughfares of Oxford Street and Regent Street much abject poverty remained.

What all the investigators showed was that the old London, reminiscent of the 1890s, was still there in the 1930s in contrast with the world of cocktails, motor cars and jazz. Although the poverty was not so horrendous or so widespread as it had been in Booth's day (the 1890s), there were still dockers out of work, sweat shops paying starvation wages in the East End, muffin men hawking in the streets, and there was still the annual exodus of hop pickers down to Kent.[4]

The West Central area of London, which was served by the Mission, came off rather better than other parts of the capital as a result of pre-war slum clearance and war-time emergency measures. In the early 1930s the percentage of persons living in poverty, i.e. short of essential requirements in food, clothing and shelter, in the western area of London had declined in the previous forty years from 29.1% to 7.8%, or by not far short of three quarters. In 1891 in Hugh Price Hughes's time, Holborn had a population of 67,000. Forty years later it was only 39,000 'owing mainly to the supercession of dwelling houses by business houses, a noteworthy example of which was the displacement of many narrow and crowded streets and alleys by the broad thoroughfare of Kingsway'. The City of Westminster also experienced a sharp drop of population from 202,000 in 1891 to 130,000 in 1931 due principally to the growth in the number of shops, offices, hotels and boarding houses. Nevertheless, there were still black spots. In the borough of Holborn a group of mean streets east of Southampton Row, including Millman Street, Old Gloucester Street and Devonshire Street, had considerable overcrowding (an average of over two persons per room) and an 'unsavoury reputation'. Bateman's Buildings, south of Soho Square, was also the scene of much squalour.[5]

An important reason for the reduction of poverty in West Central London was the operation of the Rent Restriction Acts of 1915 and 1920. Hugh Price Hughes had given as an explanation of the greater overcrowding in Holborn and Soho than in many parts of the East End the fact that rents were higher in the West End. Tenement dwellers then had less of their meagre weekly incomes available for the purchase of food and clothing. With wages rising in the war years, but rents fixed, the inhabitants of Holborn and Westminster fared better than did those of, say, Tower Hamlets, where pre-war rents were lower.

The immediate cause of much pre-war poverty and sickness was excessive drinking, which was a major social evil. It is understandable that the leaders of the Mission placed great emphasis on persuading breadwinners and others to sign the pledge. With the onset of war and the prevalence of higher earnings the problem of drunkenness was intensified. It was seriously impeding the war effort. King George V was so concerned that in April 1915 he suggested to Lloyd George, the Chancellor of the Exchequer, that he (the King) should set an example to the nation by banning the consumption of alcohol in the Royal household. Lloyd George favoured the state buying the brewers, but was frustrated by the non-conformists in his own Liberal Party who considered it immoral for the state to be in any way involved in the drink trade.[6] As an alternative he greatly increased the taxes on beer and spirits and restricted the hours of business of public houses, which, instead of opening early in the morning and staying open until midnight, were closed until lunch time, closed in the afternoon until after working hours, and closed again at ten or eleven in the evening. These restrictions, which were continued into the years of peace, played an important part in reducing drunkenness. Added to this, the public house had to face new competitors in the post-war years. In London the number of cinemas increased from 94 in 1911 to 266 in 1921.[7] By 1938 it was estimated that forty per cent of the people attended the cinema once a week and twenty-five per cent went twice a week or more.[8] Another important counter-attraction to the pub was the 'wireless'. Regular broadcasts began in 1922 and were an inducement to the worker to return home rather than to spend the evening at 'The King's Head' or 'The George'. The result was that convictions for drunkenness in England and Wales declined sharply from 188,877 in 1913 to 53,080 in 1930.[9]

These significant changes inevitably affected the pattern of activity of the Mission's Sisters, who found that new problems, particularly those of population migration in and out of London, unemployment and the break-up of families, assumed a greater importance than those associated with excessive drinking.

The housing situation of many thousands of Londoners was transformed in the inter-war period largely as the result of well-designed legislation for public authority housing, a private enterprise housing boom in the 1930s and the harnessing of electricity and gas to new labour-saving domestic appliances.[10] During the short General Election campaign which quickly followed the armistice in 1918 Lloyd George had promised 'a country fit for heroes to live in'. This clearly implied a dramatic improvement in housing conditions. In 1919 for the first time the government subsidized the construction of houses which conformed to minimum standards laid down by the newly created Ministry of Health. Under this legislation and subsequent Acts sponsored by Neville Chamberlain in 1923 and John Wheatley in 1924, more than a million houses were built, mostly for letting by the local authorities. The tenants were charged 'fair rents', based on existing wage levels and 'ability to pay', rather than economic rents, based on the cost of materials and labour and the builder's profit.[11]

In his Preface to *The Doctor's Dilemma* Bernard Shaw wrote that when a patient was too poor to pay his doctor more than eighteen pence it was useless for the doctor 'to tell him that what he or his sick child needs is not medicine, but more leisure, better clothes, better food and a better drained and ventilated house'.[12] In the later 1920s and in the 1930s more and more infants were reared in those 'better drained and ventilated houses' for which Bernard Shaw had pleaded. When they attended school, an increasing number of those who were poorly nourished were given free milk – St Helen's had pioneered this policy as early as 1899. The cost of food was falling and there was a growing understanding of the relationship between diet and health. In consequence national infant mortality rates fell from 142 per 1000 in 1900–2 to 55 per 1000 in 1938.[13]

In so far as the health of adults was better protected in the inter-war years through National Insurance Acts, the relief work of the Mission's sisters was eased. But the scope of the legislation was very imperfect. Although the number of persons covered for health insurance between 1918 and 1940 almost doubled, it remained the fact that half the population was untouched by any state scheme. By virtue of his previous contributions a working man who fell sick was entitled to receive 15s. a week health insurance and free medical treatment through his 'panel' doctor. However, the big shortcoming of the Acts was that his dependents were not entitled to receive any benefits. The assumption at the Ministry of Health was that married women living with their husbands need not be included since, where the unit was the family, it was the husband's and not the wife's health that it was important to insure.[14] A family

14. Preaching in
Hyde Park, 1906

15. Donald Soper in
Hyde Park, 1985

16. Hinde Street Church, 1887. The present headquarters of the West London Mission

17. Kingsway Hall

18.   Lake Orion Methodist Church, Michigan, USA, visited by
the Revd John Richardson and family in 1979.
The visit was reciprocated by the Revd Edward L. Duncan.

19. The Kreuzkirche, Leipzig, German Democratic Republic

20. Members of the Hinde Street and Kreuzkirche congregations at Leipzig railway station, July 1986. Pastor W. Maneck is centre at back with white shirt and wearing glasses.
The Revd Stuart Jordan (head bent sideways) is on his left.

in this situation could be worse off than if the breadwinner was unemployed. Between 1931 and the beginning of 1935 an unemployed man with a wife and three children was entitled to 29s. 3d. a week, subject to a means test, and from 1936 onwards the entitlement was raised to 36s. a week. The effect of these anomalies as between health and unemployment insurance was often to persuade the man to continue working when he ought to have reported sick.

The number of persons entitled to receive state pensions was greatly increased under Chamberlain's Widows, Orphans and Old Age Contributory Pensions Act of 1925. However, for a pensioner living alone the 10s. a week provided was often insufficient to stave off poverty; a married couple with £1 a week might just manage. The dreaded Victorian Poor Law was abolished in 1929, but the locally organized Public Assistance Committees which took the place of the Poor Law Guardians were obliged by law to apply a family means test before granting relief. For this reason many needy pensioners, not wishing to be a burden to their relations, did not ask the PACs for help, and instead endeavoured to keep up appearances on inadequate incomes.[15] These were the old men and women for whom the Mission Sisters kept a caring concern.

In sum, therefore, the calls on the Mission's resources to counteract the ravages of poverty were reduced, but were certainly not eradicated. Pockets of abysmal poverty and overcrowding in filthy tenement dwellings were still to be found within easy walking distance of Kingsway Hall. The Mission's annual report for 1929–30 gave details of a nearby street of 26 houses in which 88 families of a total of 417 persons were living in 158 rooms. In the worst case, nine persons were living in one room, but in another case, almost as horrendous, thirteen people were living in two rooms. Circumstances such as these lent urgency to the appeals to the Kingsway membership and supporters for money to maintain the Mission's social work, including the financing of slum dwellers' visits to the seaside.[16]

– II –

It was industrial changes, the varying incidence of unemployment and the resulting migration of population which gave rise to new challenges to the ministers, staff and members of the West London

Mission. In contrast with the situation in the 1890s (as outlined in Chapter 1) when the incidence of unemployment in London was the highest in the country, the 1920s and 1930s were years of relative prosperity in the capital. The centres of coal mining, heavy industry and cotton textile manufacture in South Wales, the North East, Lancashire and Scotland bore the brunt of the economic depression of the 1930s, while Greater London gained a lion's share of the new industrial development. In 1930 the percentages of the work force unemployed in some of the principal regions of the UK were as follows: London, 9.8; Midlands 18.6; North East 24.5; North West 29.5; Scotland 23.5; Wales 31.2.[17]

Although the employment situation in London as a whole was far better than it was in the old industrial centres of Britain, there were great differences between the severe hardships endured in parts of the East End and the booming activity of the western and north-western fringes. In 1933 the Medical Officer of Health of the Borough of Bethnal Green reported:

> A large section of the population has been subsisting for some years on the limited resources of unemployment benefit, public assistance and the charitable help of relatives and friends. Recent enquiries concerning nutrition go to show that the amount of assistance they receive is inadequate to maintain the families of the unemployed or low-wage workers in a proper state of health.[18]

Meanwhile on the western and north-western extremities an explosion of factory building was taking place in Park Royal, Greenford, Hayes, Harrow, Hendon and along the Great West Road, with mass production of such diverse commodities as razor blades, breakfast cereals, mattresses and motor cars. Such developments as these helped to double the built-up area of Greater London in the quarter-century before the Second World War. Another major development was the movement of the Ford Motor Company works to Dagenham from Manchester in 1927–30. As news of this industrial and urban expansion reached the provincial areas of heavy unemployment the reaction was what one might expect. Between 1918 and 1940 there was a net migration of 600,000 persons into the Greater London area. In her report on the social and redemptive work of the Mission in 1930 Katherine Price Hughes wrote: 'As never before, all roads lead to London. There never was a time when so many have imagined that London holds everything they want.'[19] Billy Rounce of Jarrow was typical of many of his age and class. The unemployment rate in his home town was sixty-seven per cent, and he had heard that in High Wycombe it was only three per cent. He was twenty-eight and had been six years unemployed. The one big difficulty was that he couldn't raise the money for the rail fare. So he bought a platform ticket at Newcastle Central Station and boarded the train for King's Cross, where he was met by a friend with two of that station's platform tickets. He knew that one-time citizens of Jarrow were scattered all over London but that there was a recognized meeting place for those in trouble, or merely seeking companionship. It was the seventh lamp post on the path from Speakers' Corner southwards to Hyde Park Corner.[20]

To her comments on London in 1930 Katherine Price Hughes might have added another sentence: 'Never before has there been such movement of peoples within Greater London.' On tubes, buses and trams the average Londoner took 210 rides a year in 1911 and 388 in 1938. It was a situation which arose partly as a result of the new job opportunities opening up on the fringes but also as a result of the London County Council's large-scale and successful efforts to rehouse the slum dwellers and others from the inner city in cottage estates, or estates of flats in locations such as White Hart Lane (1921–8), St Helier near Wimbledon (1930–2) and Downham, near Lewisham (1925–30). Although the housing conditions of the thousands who moved were transformed, most of the wage earners in the new estates lived a long way from their work. Thus less than a quarter of the inhabitants of Watling (who had been moved out from King's Cross, St Pancras and Islington) worked in nearby Hendon; over a half of them worked in central London. Hence, although their working day had been reduced by an hour after the war, this was more than offset by increased travelling time, since to qualify for a cheap 'workman's' ticket they had to leave Burnt Oak underground station by 7.30 a.m. Another consequence of the movement of people to the outer suburbs was the decline of population of Holborn and Westminster referred to above. It also meant a reduction in the number of potential worshippers in the Mission's churches from the immediate neighbourhood. A longer journey to work meant more meals out. From the time that the first

Joe Lyons tea shop was opened in Piccadilly in 1894, the business expanded rapidly until by the end of the 1920s it had opened 250 such establishments nationally. The Londoner who wanted to give his wife a special treat would, as likely as not, take her to one of the three Lyons Corner Houses in London, each of which could seat up to 3,000 persons and in each of which live music was played. These huge establishments were not necessarily counter-attractions to church attendance; worshippers often visited them after attending a service in the morning or evening.

– III –

A comparison of the Annual Report of the Mission for 1932 with that of 1900 reveals the way in which rapid changes in government social policy, the employment situation and the distribution of London population affected the Mission's priorities in social work. The report for 1900, after listing the religious services indoors and in the open air, gives pride of place to temperance work: 'At each Hall a Temperance Society, a Temperance Legion and a Band of Hope.' This is followed by 'district visiting by Sisters, Missioners and Volunteer staff and the organization of "Room to Room Guilds"; slate clubs, penny banks, clothing, provident and boot clubs; a servant's registry and men's labour bureau; two dispensaries; a crèche; a home of peace for the dying; a Guild of Poor Brave Things and Workhouse teas.' Only then, near the bottom of the lists, comes the item 'Rescue Work'.

In 1932 there is no mention of temperance work or slate clubs, boot clubs or penny banks. The nationally organized labour exchanges had largely done away with the need for a servant's registry and men's labour bureau. With the expansion of health insurance the dispensaries had been closed, and 'workhouse teas' get no mention as the workhouse had been abolished in 1929. The home of peace for the dying had passed out of control of the Mission in 1911 and the 'Guild of the Poor Brave Things' had become the 'Guild of the Brave Comrades'. On the other hand there is a full-page report on the work of the Sisters visiting the sick, the disabled and the needy, and the continuing value of the crèche and second-hand clothes store is rightly stressed. Significant new developments noted are 'the large numbers of men who have come to London seeking work' and the comment: 'The time that has been given to the need of this particular type would be almost incredible. It seemed sometimes as if the Mission were invaded.' The most remarkable change is the prominence given to two post-war ventures: the Sister Mabel Hostel for girls stranded in London and in need of care and supervision was set up in Drury Lane in 1921 and the Parkhurst Maternity Hospital was founded in 1923.

The war not only opened up hundreds of thousands of job opportunities for women, it also accelerated their advance towards greater independence in their life style, manners and dress. In May 1915 the *Daily Mail* commented: 'Just now our young and pretty girls are pushing the craze for short skirts to the utmost limit.' Make-up was commonly used by women on the European continent before 1914, but, apart from the use of face powder, it was virtually unknown in Britain.[21] By the early 1920s the use of lipstick and eye shadow was widespread, not only in London but throughout the country. After the armistice, although the strongest pressure was used to persuade women to relinquish those jobs they had taken over from men, they were not easily persuaded to abandon their quest for economic independence. With job prospects in London brighter than elsewhere, women as well as men flocked to the capital from every part of the kingdom. As one of the hopefuls expressed it in 1927: 'You see, Sister, you can get more money in London for doing less work, than you can in the North.'[22] However, many of those who burned their boats and cut themselves off from their families were in their late teens and very inexperienced. If they failed to find the work they expected they could soon be destitute and open to manifold temptations. There were thousands of women and young girls in this plight in London between the wars.

The establishment of the Sister Mabel Hostel in Drury Lane on 8 May 1921 owed much to the initiative of Sister Mabel (who died shortly after the hostel's opening) and of Dr J. E. Rattenbury. On 17 January 1921 Rattenbury met Major Cyril Bavin of the Red Triangle Hospitality League, an offshoot of the YMCA, which employed patrols to seek out girls who were in danger of drifting into prostitution and gave them shelter, food and guidance in its Drury Lane premises. The result of the two leaders' conversation was that the Mission acquired the hostel, on lease, free of rent, on the understanding that the Mission should provide the matron and staff for the new hostel and that the League should nominate one representative to the management committee.[23] Up to March 1936 more than 8,500 girls were received into the hostel on short stay.[24] They came from all over Britain. In the twelve months to 31 March 1931, for example, girls entered the hostel from sixty-three towns in England, Wales, Scotland and both parts of Ireland.[25] Some were referred to Sister Bertha (who managed the hostel) by the police, some were found by the Sisters in Hyde Park, some came of their own initiative. They came because they were destitute; because they were pregnant and had nowhere to go; because they were sacked from employment in hotels and restaurants or as maids in private homes or because they had been referred to the hostel by magistrates. Although the work of Sister Bertha was invaluable, the thirty beds available were grossly inadequate compared with the need. The drawbacks of limited space were emphasized in the report for 1930:

> The Sister Mabel Hostel does not meet the insistent urgent needs of the hour. Newcomers must be admitted, and so before the work of reclamation is consolidated, the girl passes on – probably to lodgings – and long before she ought, she is once again in the midst of temptation.[26]

It was for reasons of this kind that Katherine Price Hughes wrote in 1928: 'The time has come when we must have more accommodation. During the coming year we shall have to open another hostel where girls who demand more care and protection than can be given in our present premises, will be received and cared for.'[27] But although a separate fund was started and substantial donations were received it was difficult to find appropriate accommodation, and it was not until 1937 that the Katherine Price Hughes Hostel was opened at No. 8 Doughty Street, WC1.

Wartime circumstances led to increased promiscuity among men and women. In the early 1920s there was concern about the spread of venereal disease just as in the 1980s alarm has grown about the incidence of AIDS. To meet this new challenge, in 1923 the Mission began a new undertaking, the Parkhurst Maternity Hospital, 'a double fronted corner house with an old fashioned garden at the back', in Parkhurst Road near Holloway Prison. The medical profession had discovered that by a course of ante-natal treatment mothers affected by VD could be cured and their babies born healthy. Sister Faull, who was in charge of the hospital, made arrangements with the staff of the Royal Free Hospital for the regular treatment of the expectant mothers in her care. The results were extremely gratifying. By 1936 238 babies were born at Parkhurst, almost all of them perfectly healthy.[28] It was Sister Faull's testimony that almost all the mothers were 'won' to love their babies. This was no doubt a common experience, but nevertheless one which helped to make the work of the staff at Parkhurst enjoyable.

The principal extension of the work of the crèche in these years was the acquisition of 'Hopedene' high up in Barnet, North London, in 1919, as a holiday home for children who were sickly and severely undernourished. The air was delightfully fresh and the children made giant strides towards recovery through being well fed and lovingly cared for by the nurses. The main work of the crèche continued on the extensive sixth floor of Kingsway. In the 1920s and early 1930s an average of over 10,000 attendances was recorded each year with over fifty children being admitted daily. In the later 1930s some thirty children a day were being cared for. Mrs Winnie Wintringham (née Hinde) has recalled that when she was a senior staff nurse at the crèche, between 1937 and 1940, the mothers were 'from the manual working class' and that the services provided 'were vital to the mothers and their families'. The majority of the children 'were very undernourished and poorly clad' and many of them were supplied with clothing for their general use. Sister Hope, who gave forty-four years of service to the crèche, died in 1936, to be succeeded by Sister Lawrence, who took charge of the four trained staff. The senior staff nurses' salary was £1 a week with full board and with deduction of 2s. 6d. a week for insurance. Mrs Wintringham considered that, as far as her pay was concerned, 'the element of giving one's services was still there'.[29]

With the rapid spread of the communications network – more tube and bus routes, more private motor cars – quicker getaway was possible for the criminal. The prison population was increasing. The Mission met this challenge by systematic prison visiting, particularly of Holloway. The 1931 annual reports noted that 'twice a week one of the sisters visits Holloway Prison'. On prisoners' discharge one of the Sisters 'meets them at the prison gates, finds shelter for the homeless, and where possible work for the unemployed'. The Sisters were also represented on the Discharged Prisoners' Aid Committee.[30] These responsibilities entailed an immense amount of work. In 1935 over 400 visits were made to prisoners, fifty early morning services for women prisoners were conducted, and fifty meetings of committees dealing with the welfare of discharged prisoners were attended.[31] In early 1938 the new Superintendent, Dr Donald O. Soper, took this valuable work a stage further by opening a hostel for ex-prisoners in a side street off the Strand.[32]

– IV –

In September 1925 Dr J. E. Rattenbury ended his very distinguished eighteen-year tenure as Superintendent of the West London Mission. Many years of active Christian life remained before his death at the age of ninety-one on 19 January 1963. He was elected President of the Free Church Council in 1936 and was President of the Methodist Sacramental Fellowship from 1939–50. He was opposed to the terms on which the United Methodist Church was formed in 1932 because he favoured a wider expression of ecumenism. He was welcomed back to Kingsway and Hinde Street from time to time in the post-war era when for some years he was listed among the Mission's team of ministers.

His immediate successor as Superintendent in September 1925 was C. Francis Ream, who was born in Grantham and attended schools there before winning a scholarship to Cambridge. Before coming to Kingsway he gained mission hall experience at Archway Road (North London) (1916–19), Manchester (1919–21) and Stockport (1921–5). It was a tragedy that he died suddenly within six months of his return to London and therefore had insufficient time to leave his mark on the Mission's work.

The Revd Ira G. Goldhawk, who was Superintendent for ten years from 1926, was born at Kimberton in Hertfordshire. Unlike his successor Dr Donald Soper, he had a village, rather than an urban background; but he did have eight years as Superintendent at the Albert Hall, Nottingham, before coming to Kingsway. He found delight in simple things and had a genuine concern for secular activities, such as golf, music and reading. His theology was described as a simple Methodist piety 'which came from a sense of wonder at the mystery of our great Christian redemption'. He believed in the centrality of the preached word. He was said to be a 'master of the pregnant pause', but he had a gift of humour and for making the congregation feel they were in dialogue with him. The Revd F. W. Newland, MA, who attended one of his services at Kingsway Hall in December 1929, recorded his impressions as follows:

> When the half hour of attractive music was over I could perceive hardly any vacant seats. I noticed many working people and a large number of young folk. As soon as Mr Ira G. Goldhawk followed the choir and the Sisters to the platform it was obvious that he held the congregation in the hollow of his hand and was able to play upon them at his will. Homely illustrations, seasoned with irresistible humour, brightened a timely discourse which included again and again a sudden home thrust. I felt I was in a great mixed assembly, thoroughly at home.[33]

Although Goldhawk introduced no major innovations in the Mission's social work he gave conscientious support to the activities already established. In view of his great abilities as a preacher, it is not surprising that the Kingsway membership figures were well sustained at between 530 and 590 during the years he was in charge. Membership in the Mission as a whole, including the societies at Hinde Street, King's Cross and Hyde Park, rose from 1,084 in 1929 to 1,118 in 1935.[34]

Dr Donald O. Soper, who became Superintendent of the West London Mission in 1936, was the youngest man ever to be appointed to the post. It had been customary to expect that whoever took charge of a central mission of the importance of that at Kingsway Hall would have served at least twenty years as an ordained minister. Soper had completed only eleven years of the expected twenty, but was nevertheless appointed because of his outstanding qualities.

He was born at 36 Knoll Road, Wandsworth, on 31 January 1903, but spent the greater part of his boyhood in Streatham. He came of a family in every respect well endowed. It was comfortably off through the fact that his father was an average adjuster of the City of London while his mother was a teacher and later a headmistress. It was well endowed culturally and intellectually since meal times were characterized by the cut and thrust of informed discussion and were often followed by musical evenings in which all took part. Both parents were ardent Methodists, giving unequivocal guidance on moral issues. Only a few hundred yards from the Soper household hundreds of families were living in abject poverty, but it was perfectly possible in those pre-1914 days for middle-class families to be largely unaware how the 'other half' lived.

At Aske's School, Hatcham in 1918 Donald Soper passed the army gymnastic staff examination with an essay on 'The Spirit of the Bayonet'. At the time he found this training 'entirely proper and exciting'. But when he kept rooms at St Catherine's College, Cambridge, and met as fellow students ex-soldiers, older than himself, whose limbs had been mutilated or whose bodies had rotted in the trenches, he came to regard his former 'martial exercises' as an 'obscenity' and he concluded that war was wholly contrary to the spirit of Christ.[35] Shortly afterwards he visited the railway workshops in Derby, his first visit to a factory and first contact with factory workers. It was a 'revelation'. It brought to him a new significance of the lawyer's question 'Who is my neighbour?' in the Parable of the Good Samaritan. More than any other single experience it helped to make him a Socialist.[36]

When Donald Soper came to Kingsway from Islington Central Hall in 1936 he already had a reputation as a pacifist and socialist.

> Some then imagined that the life at Kingsway Hall would now be like an Adult School or a Labour Party Sunday School mixed with a heckling session.[37]

They were quite shocked by the actual nature of the worship, 'which was most carefully liturgical, and by the preaching which was Bible based'. Leonard Barnett, who heard him in the autumn of 1936, summed it up well when he wrote that 'he pleaded a Gospel based on the love of God in Christ and related to our daunting world scene'. It was a 'full orbed Gospel of personal and social redemption'.[38]

11

The War Years 1939–45

The shadow of the Second World War fell over the life and activities of the West London Mission some time before the declaration of war on Germany on 3 September 1939. Almost a year earlier, on 25 September 1938, following the Munich crisis, the ARP services were mobilized, cellars and basements were requisitioned for air raid shelters, trenches were dug in the public parks and 28 million gas masks were issued to men, women and children (but none to babies). Young men members of Dick Sheppard's Peace Pledge Union, who had been attracted to Kingsway Hall by the uncompromising pacifism of Donald Soper, had their faith and convictions severely tested following the passing of the Military Training Act in May 1939, conscripting young men of twenty and twenty-one. Those of that group who believed that military service was incompatible with their Christian faith were among the first of the 60,000 men and women who registered as conscientious objectors during the war years. On 1 September 1939, two days before the declaration of war, there was a mass evacuation of mothers, children and babies from the larger urban areas to the country districts. A double-decker bus arrived outside Kingsway Hall at eight o'clock that morning to take twenty-seven crèche children, all under five years of age, Sister Mary and the five nursery staff to the Methodist schoolroom in St Albans, pending their accommodation in a large house in that city.[1]

On the first day of the war the Sunday morning services at both Kingsway Hall and Hinde Street were interrupted at 11.27 by the wail of the sirens signalling an 'alert' and the ministers and congregations descended into the Masonic Hall basement in Great Queen Street and into the Hinde Street Church basement for shelter, many imagining that this was the beginning of an all-out assault on the capital. However, that first 'alert' of the war was a false alarm. There followed the period of the 'phoney war' to the end of August 1940, when London was largely free of air raids while the Luftwaffe was engaged in giving air support to the German invasions of Poland, Denmark, Norway, Belgium and Northern France. Most of the evacuees, including the staff and children of the crèche, returned to London at least for some months, until the air assault on the capital began in earnest. In these early days of the war it was the blackout which was the greatest inconvenience, restricting social activity, including attendance at evening worship, by the elderly and more cautious members of the community. The hospitals, prepared for conducting major surgery in the wake of massive bombing raids, were, instead, kept busy dealing with accidents caused by people stumbling or falling in the darkness.

The period of phoney war came to an abrupt end on 24 August 1940 with the first heavy night raid on London. The systematic bombing of the city began in early September and then the raiders appeared for fifty-seven consecutive nights. There was no let-up for Londoners until 11 May 1941, when the German bombers were diverted to the east in support of Hitler's 'Operation Barbarossa': the invasion of the USSR. It was then the turn of the Russian people to undergo much more widespread devastation and suffering than even the hard-pressed civilian populations of Britain had endured in the Blitz. The lull in the bombing of London continued until January 1944, when a 'Little Blitz' began, lasting three months. After another brief lull, the final and in some ways the most terrifying phase of the aerial war, that of the flying bombs, came between June 1944 and March 1945. The route of the piloted bomber, whose targets had been lit up by incendiaries dropped by pathfinder planes, could generally be predicted. The attacks of the flying bombs, by comparison, seemed completely inhuman and capricious.[2]

It is difficult for anyone who did not live through the experience to recapture the immensity of the fire and bomb assault on London, and particularly the Dockland area, on nights such as 7–8 September 1940. Vera Brittain recorded that 'from different angles, at different heights, and with different speeds came fifteen hundred aeroplanes of all types and sizes dropping bombs by the ton in eight hours of terror'.[3] Barbara Nixon, who was a command post warden in the West End, wrote of the same night, that 'in Shaftesbury Avenue, five miles from the blaze, it was possible to read the evening paper'.[4] In peacetime any fire which required the attendance of thirty pumps was regarded as very big indeed; but on that night there were nine huge fires that engaged 100 pumps each, nineteen that required thirty or more, forty needing ten pumps each and nearly a thousand lesser fires requiring fewer than ten pumps.[5] Some nights later, in that first phase of the Blitz, the bombers also attacked the West End. Famous department stores including John Lewis's, Bourne and Hollingsworth's and Walpole's were gutted and 'Bond Street had almost as good a claim as Bow Road to be considered a devastated area'.[6]

The spread of air raids to the west directly affected the Hinde Street and Kingsway Hall communities. Although the typical householder generally complied with official instructions and took pictures off walls, placed buckets of sand in passageways and filled the bath – if there was one – with water, he or she often preferred to take refuge in a deep shelter. Both churches had deep basements which were sandbagged and which were used by the staff of the Mission, by people who had been bombed out of their homes, and sometimes by nearby residents simply seeking better shelter. At Hinde Street, the minister in charge, the Revd W. G. Salmon, led a team of fire watchers who slept in the basement during off-duty hours.[7] A 'public shelter committee' of the church held its first meeting on 1 July 1940, when its members were informed that the basement of the church had been designated an ARP C5 post and that it was to be made available as a temporary shelter to those who had been bombed out of their homes. At the height of the Blitz in September 1940 nearly 100 persons were being accommodated each night; but generally there were fewer than half that number of shelterers. The congregation of the church responded generously to the minister's appeal for blankets and cooking utensils while the LCC gave financial assistance.[8] The church itself had two narrow escapes from serious damage from air raids. The top stone of the spire, which had been placed in position with much ceremony over fifty years earlier, rose bodily under the impact of a nearby explosion, but returned to its correct position. Had it fallen on the roof, the damage could have been substantial. For safety's sake it had to be removed and was not replaced until 1953. In another raid an incendiary bomb penetrated the church roof unobserved. One of the roof beams was ignited and the flames died out within inches of the plaster above the organ.[9]

It was fortunate that Kingsway Hall, the headquarters of the Mission, though hit by incendiaries, largely escaped bomb damage. It was not one of the 2,600 Methodist churches (out of a total of 9,000 in Britain) severely damaged during the war.[10] This left the staff and voluntary workers free to help relieve the distress and discomfort which was much in evidence in the neighbourhood. In autumn 1940 the extensive basement area of the hall was designated by the LCC as a Rest and Feeding Centre. There were heavy air raids on the night of its opening and 200 bombed-out people found their temporary home with the caretakers and off-duty firewatchers of the Mission.[11]

In December 1939 the London Passenger Transport Board posted notices at all its underground stations warning the public that the premises were not to be used as air raid shelters. This directive was largely followed until 7 September 1940, when, during hours of intense bombardment, thousands of Londoners defied it and flocked to the platforms with their bedding and other essential belongings. To give an air of legality to their action they bought platform tickets costing 1½d. each. It was not long before the LPTB bowed to the inevitable, removed the ban, and even authorized the issuance of platform season tickets. At the height of the Blitz seventy-nine stations, with fifteen miles of platform, were occupied each night by some 177,000 persons. Disused stations at South Kentish Town, British Museum and City Road were handed over to the local authorities for use as shelters. Although enough bunks were provided in the tube stations to accommodate 22,000 persons, most of those taking refuge preferred to lie on their blankets on the platforms – it seemed less isolated and 'snooty'. In the course of time fifty-two lending libraries were functioning for the benefit of this nocturnal multitude. Soft drinks, meat pies, sausage rolls, pasties, apple turnovers and buns could be purchased on the platforms of the larger stations. One group of shelterers even established its own newspaper, *The Swiss Cottager*.[12]

One of the more commodious stations was Holborn, just across the road from Kingsway Hall. Between 6 and 8.30 each week-day morning hundreds of men and women shelterers emerged into Kingsway looking weary, peckish and unkempt. Undoubtedly one of the greatest services which the Sisters and their volunteer helpers in the Mission performed for Londoners during the Blitz was to open a breakfast canteen on 2 October 1940 and to keep it open each working day from 6.00 till 8.00 a.m., until 1 December 1944, when it was less urgently needed since three cafés had opened in the neighbourhood. The canteen served an average of 700 breakfasts a week at the modest charge of 1s. 3d. for fruit juice, cereal, bacon and egg, and a cup of tea. Not all of those who came for the meal were persuaded they were getting good value for their money. One morning when Dr Soper, dressed in mufti, was at the cash desk, a worldly-wise customer leaned over to him with a knowing wink and said, 'I bet the minister here is making a packet out of this'. One reporter, emerging into the daylight from Holborn tube station, asked a passer-by where he might get a bite to eat. He was advised to go to Kingsway Hall. 'You'll get a shave and wash there too. They'll set you up for work down there.'[13]

Lunches and teas, as well as breakfasts, were served at Kingsway Hall during the war years. The Mission acquired such a good reputation for the provision of meals that the Ministry of Food contacted Donald Soper in September 1942 to discover whether some of the Kingsway staff or volunteers would be available to help sort out and allocate supplies of surplus food stored in Covent Garden. The big problem was how to transport these 'tired vegetables' to Kingsway Hall and other feeding centres. Petrol was strictly rationed and in short supply. However, when Soper telephoned the fuel controller's office he discovered that the man answering the call was a contemporary of his at school. There were then no further difficulties about fuel permits and the vegetables reached their various destinations before they were too tired to be fit for consumption.[14]

– II –

The blackout, the evacuation of many office workers, school children and their mothers inevitably resulted in smaller congregations at Sunday services. In the Spring 1940 edition of *Kingsway Chronicle* Donald Soper wrote of 'congregations evacuated, coffers depleted, subscriptions halved, such is part, the inevitable part, of the story of Kingsway Hall during the past six months'. However, the impact of the war on the Hinde Street congregations was more severe. In contrast with the congregations at Kingsway Hall, which contained a large element of single people, many of whom were 'passing through' London, those of Hinde Street contained a larger element of established family groups living in the West End or in London's outer suburbs. Evacuation took away a bigger proportion of the worshippers than was the case at Kingsway. Church membership at Hinde Street, which was 180 in the last year of peace, fell to 145 in 1942 and 107 in 1947. Wartime congregations averaged about forty persons for each service, a figure less than half that of peace time.[15] Kingsway congregations fluctuated with the intensity or absence of aerial bombardment. In the period of phoney war more than 2,000 people attended the Sunday services, and on 10 March 1940 fifty-six new members were received into the church.[16] In the middle of the Blitz Donald Soper reported that 'numbers have been affected but the Fellowship was very real'.[17] 'A steady increase in congregations' was noted in August 1942 when the Luftwaffe was concentrated on the Eastern Front.[18] When the 'Little Blitz' came in January 1944 attendances were 'disappointingly small', and when in the following month a spell of intense cold accompanied the heavy bombings the Sunday congregations were 'not too good'.[19] During the period of the flying bombs in the summer of 1944 it was decided to concentrate the congregations under the balconies 'as a precaution against broken glass during raids', but the Superintendent found preaching difficult under these circumstances.[20]

It is not surprising that flying bombs had the most serious deterrent effect on church attendances. On weekdays they were timed to arrive as Londoners were on their way to work, and on Sundays the arrival time was 'eleven o'clock . . . when either church or morning stroll might find people congregated or on the streets'. One of the worst incidents of the war occurred on 18 June 1944 when a flying bomb hit the Guards' Chapel in Wellington Barracks during the morning service, killing 119 people and seriously injuring 102.[21]

From Passion Sunday in March 1942 Donald Soper conducted open air meetings in Hyde Park as well as the morning and evening services in Kingsway Hall. Since the speaker never disguised his pacifism, the heckling in the Park was often unremitting and remorseless. At various times the meetings were described as 'tumultuous', 'hard', 'somewhat hectic' and 'not good'.[22] Inevitably the speaker's voice was affected. On Monday mornings it was said to resemble that of 'a dying corncrake'. At a Local Preachers' Meeting in Kingsway Hall in September 1942 Mr Clee 'questioned the wisdom of Dr Soper continuing these meetings, as he considered the strain of two services and one open air meeting on a single day was detrimental to Dr Soper's health'. The questioner did not know his Superintendent. The open air controversy was what Donald Soper most enjoyed. In reply to Mr Clee he said that 'although he appreciated his concern, he felt that the work in Hyde Park was an urgent duty which he could not and would not neglect'.[23] And there were compensations. The Spring 1944 issue of *Kingsway Chronicle* reported: 'It gladdens our hearts to see Sunday afternoon hecklers becoming Sunday evening worshippers at Kingsway Hall.'

– III –

The social work of the West London Mission was continued and even extended in the course of the Second World War. The Men's Hostel in Drury Lane near the Strand had been opened in 1938 after Donald Soper and Stanley Shaw had considered the project when they met in the Discharged Prisoners' Aid Committee. They saw the need for a home for discharged prisoners while they found work and re-established themselves as useful citizens. The hostel was not a large one; but it accommodated about fifty men each year for varying periods of residence, while over the same span of time advice and help was given to nearly 1,000 callers. In 1942 the Pilgrim Trust donated £300 towards the work of the hostel, at that time being managed by ex-constable Percy Hubbard of Y Division, Metropolitan Police.[24] In 1941 the director of the Association concerned with the welfare of prisoners who had served long periods of detention in Dartmoor or Parkhurst prisons wrote:

> One reads of efforts now being made to salvage old iron, tins and kitchen refuse, but what about the human salvage on our doorsteps? Your work at the West London Mission is a light shining in the wilderness, and deserves wider recognition.

The claim of the Mission at the time was that out of 1,500 men that had been under its care since the hostel was opened, only fifty-two had gone back to prison.[25]

London magistrates, appalled at the growth of delinquency of all kinds among young shelterers, were constantly urging the establishment of mixed recreational centres. The Kingsway Club made a small contribution to meeting this need. It provided facilities for table tennis, billiards, games and gymnastics and also offered classes and refreshments; it had a membership in 1941 of 187, with an average attendance of 80, three or four times a week.[26] The Katherine Price Hughes Hostel at 8 Doughty Street with accommodation for up to fifteen girls 'in need of care and supervision' was full and busy throughout the war. On Monday nights it provided an 'indoor Tower Hill' when Donald Soper came to answer questions. He declared that 'open air Tower Hill was easy' compared with the gruelling he received in Doughty Street.[27] The second-hand clothing depot at 37 Grafton Way was also kept open through the war, fulfilling a new kind of need. In 1944 it was reported that the depot was 'besieged by anxious callers after each raid'.[28] The crèche continued to function during the war years, although the comings and goings of the Luftwaffe resulted in its location changing between Kingsway and St Albans. In 1943 the Ministry of Health ruled that Holborn Borough Council should assume financial responsibility for the work. This was not a decision which was welcomed by the Mission, which was glad to resume full responsibility for the service from 1 October 1945.[29]

The provision of a Christmas dinner for needy and lonely people was a tradition established from the earliest days of the Mission. On 26 December 1887 'a good old fashioned Christmas dinner', with music and games to follow, was provided at 60 Greek Street, Soho.[30] Food rationing in the war years and for some time after made it impossible to maintain this festivity on its peacetime scale, but a meal and entertainment were provided for a limited number each year.

In the months following the Battle of Britain in 1940, when air raids caused the number of civilian casualties greatly to exceed those on the battlefronts, the common danger crowded together in shelters men and women who in peacetime would never have dreamed of associating together. It would have been hard to find a more independent-minded collection of people than the nightly occupants of the seats on the Thames Embankment. The entry into the community of these vagrants came with the first night-time bombings. Much to the embarrassment of the wardens, who were well aware of their verminous condition, they resorted to the public shelters. When the wardens tried to isolate them in corners and in side aisles, a group of some fifty of them took refuge in Arch 173 underneath Charing Cross main line station. A contemporary described the 'macabre and noisome' scene that was then created:

> The vagrants lit seven or eight open fires, and looking into the arch at night, a tall dark-ceilinged cavernous place, Dickensian, and in the same gloomy Hungerford Lane where Dickens himself spent his boyhood of the blacking factory – one saw only haunches and lower torsos squatting round the red fires, for the heads were long lost in a pall of smoke that hung down and filled the tall arch from its ceiling.

The Westminster City Council decided that what was happening under Arch 173 constituted a risk to public health. It resolved to transform another of the Charing Cross arches into a combined cleansing and welfare centre. Baths, bunks, a canteen and a first aid post were installed. Canon T. B. Scrutton, the Revd Paul Gliddon and members of the Anglican Peace Fellowship and Fellowship of Reconciliation from St Martins-in-the-Fields and Kingsway Hall agreed to run the new establishment, which they called the Hungerford Club. It opened on 26 February 1941. The first job was to de-louse the club members. Of the 4,500 destitute persons who came and went in the course of the war very few were not infested. All those who *were*, especially the record holder with 15,000 lice on his person, contributed handsomely to the public welfare, for the lice gathered at the club were forwarded to laboratories, such as the one at the School of Hygiene and Tropical Medicine, to further the cause of medical research.

When stocks of lice ran low as a result of the successful efforts of the cleansing department, some members of the staff volunteered to let the lice breed on their own bodies in order to maintain essential supplies.[31] When in May 1944 the Hungerford Club was in danger of collapsing since some of its sponsors and volunteer workers considered that the need for it was less urgent, others of the workers appealed to Donald Soper to intervene to save the venture. Soper told a meeting of the Club's managing committee on 3 May that 'he was prepared to take a practical interest if the necessary funds for the undertaking were forthcoming'. By January 1945, the LCC having given a promise of financial support, he announced that the club had been taken over by the Mission and had been incorporated in its social work. Then in the autumn of that year the LCC granted Kingsway Hall the use of the old casual ward of Lambeth Workhouse at a rental of £50 a year, and by the end of February 1946 the site in the Charing Cross arches was vacated and the new home for the club was opened.[32] That there was a need for the club was shown by the fact that between sixty and seventy men slept in the (revamped) Wincott Street premises each night.[33]

— IV —

The BBC had banned Donald Soper from broadcasting, but his advocacy of the gospel message spread far and wide throughout the kingdom in the war years. The essential message was grasped by Leonard Barnett, whose character as a Methodist minister was largely shaped by what he heard at Kingsway Hall and on Tower Hill. He learnt that to be a Christian meant personal commitment to Christ *and* the inescapable commitment to Christianize the environment at every point. What had great appeal was,

> the insight of the Bible as a whole and the life and teaching of Jesus Christ in particular, in the light of the week's headlines and the relationship between the two which came up week by week freshly minted, vital, topical, to earn acceptance in the minds of the congregation.[34]

A large book of cuttings from local newspapers in the possession of the Mission reveals that Donald Soper was much in demand as a speaker throughout the war years. His speeches were positive, stressing what he believed should be the nature of British society transformed in conformity with Christian principles. Speaking to an audience of 'about 2,000' at the Dome, Brighton, in February 1941 on the subject 'Each Man's Just Share' he claimed that 'every man is entitled to the fullest share in the good things of life'.[35] In St John's Methodist Church, St Austell, Cornwall in April that year he said that 'the cult of individualism, the attempt to isolate, was the supreme sin of man in his corporate life. They were God's family and it was only by living together as a family that they would live together in peace, equanimity and concord.'[36] At Walsall in November 1942 he stressed the same theme: 'Fellowship is living together, which means sharing. If you disregard the economic factor you miss one of the primary factors of fellowship.'[37] The secret of his appeal as a speaker was that his words matched what people were learning from their wartime experience of helping each other out in times of privation, of seeing the essential fairness of rationing, of appreciating the great benefits of a medical service available to all, and so on. Professor R. Titmuss, a leading social scientist of the time, maintained that 'the circumstances of the Second World War created an unprecedented sense of social solidarity among the British people, which made them accept a great increase in egalitarian policies and collectivist state intervention'.[38] Even if Titmuss's claim is only partly true, as more recent writers have claimed,[39] it does help to explain the warm rapport which was evident between Donald Soper and his audiences in places as far apart as Sheffield and Swansea, Derby and Gwennap Pit.

Furthermore Donald Soper was by no means the only churchman emphasising the need for a new social order. On 7 January 1941 a notable gathering of clergy and laity met at Malvern College under the chairmanship of William Temple,

> to consider from the Anglican point of view what are the fundamental facts which are directly relevant to the ordering of the new society that is quite evidently emerging, and how Christian thought can be shaped to play a leading part in reconstruction after the war is over.

In the statement which was issued after the conclusion of the discussions it was admitted that changes in the structure of society could never be 'self sufficient means of salvation'. Nevertheless there were 'stumbling blocks' which made it more difficult for people to live Christian lives. Among these stumbling blocks was 'the ownership of the principal industrial resources of the community – vested in the hands of private owners'.[40]

An ecumenical approach to the problem of the Christian reordering of society was revealed in a letter to *The Times* printed just before Christmas 1940. It was signed by Cardinal Hinsley, the Roman Catholic, the two Anglican Archbishops, Lang (Canterbury) and Temple (York), and the Moderator of the Free Church Federal Council. It advocated five principles to be followed: 1. Extreme inequality in wealth and possessions should be abolished; 2. All citizens should have equal educational opportunities; 3. The family must be safeguarded; 4. The sense of divine vocation must be restored to man's daily work; and 5. The resources of the earth should be used as God's gifts to the whole human race and used with due consideration for the needs of present and future generations. This programme was in full accord with the objectives of the West London Mission and had the support of its Superintendent and other ministers.[41]

– V –

The 'power house' of the work based on Kingsway Hall was the Thursday evening Guild. Each week there was a short devotional meeting made up of biblical or devotional study, some hymns, meditation and prayer. It was also the occasion for discussing plans for the future. Some young people from this group maintained a short weekly open air service at the corner of Kingsway and Parker Street half an hour before the evening service started in Kingsway Hall. Towards the end of 1941, when these outdoor services had been continuing for some weeks, Donald Soper posed this question to the members of the Guild. 'What do you think of sending out small groups of people from Kingsway into Essex and other places round London on preaching campaigns?' The appeal met a ready response from some two dozen young people present.

From this group was formed the 'Kingsway Preachers', who went into training for this new task in the early months of 1942. Donald Soper gave them instruction in the distinctive art of open air speaking as contrasted with the delivery of sermons within closed walls. Different tasks were assigned to the members according to their varying talents, and contributions to expenses were pooled and placed in a conical shaped wooden box. The evangelistic campaigns were organized on a communal, rather than an individualistic, basis.

The first campaign was held in Dorking, Surrey, for a week beginning Wednesday 27 August 1942. One reason for this 'stockbroker belt' town being chosen was that earlier that year an interdenominational body called Dorking Christian Youth had been formed and had contemplated holding a week's mission in the area. However, they were short of speakers and approached the Methodist minister, the Revd Erastus Evans, who put them in touch with the West London Mission. Thus three groups of Kingsway Preachers spread themselves out along the main street of the town and conducted open air meetings on seven consecutive evenings. A large number of the campaigners continued with their usual work, travelling up to London after breakfast each morning and returning for the meetings in Dorking in the evening.

As might have been expected of a group of young men and women coming from Kingsway in 1942, most of its members, but not all, were pacifists. They were conducting an evangelical campaign; but it was one with a difference. They believed that the gospel of Christ needed to be expressed in economic, social and political terms, as well as in the terms of personal salvation. The exuberant and joyful spirit which pervaded the week's activities was recaptured by one of the chief participants when he wrote:

> Whether it was in the delight that the campaigners experienced on becoming mixed up in a full scale Civil Defence exercise one evening, or having to contend with a thunderstorm on another occasion; whether it was in the hilarity at the meal table, particularly over Dr Soper's predilection for a homemade processed cheese that was provided for us; whether it was in the preference for singing secular songs around the schoolroom piano, rather than pious hymns, or in the last night celebration, a late walk up the Nower, marked by suitably effervescent behaviour; somehow that extraordinary combination of gaiety, and even of frivolity, with a deeply felt concern to serve Christ and His Kingdom had already been achieved.[42]

The first campaign was conducted entirely in the open air; but those of the later years of the war at Liskeard, Cornwall in 1942, Hayes, Middlesex in 1943 and Barnstable, Devon in 1944, comprised a mixture of indoor and open air meetings arranged with the co-operation of local churches.

Early in 1945 Donald Soper wrote a letter of invitation to all Methodist ministers in the London area, inviting them to a conference at Kingsway Hall in February to consider the broadening of the basis of the campaigns. The outcome was the creation of a more widely representative organization. This assumed the name of the London Christian Campaigners, into which the Kingsway Preachers merged. The first adventure of the newly formed 'Campaigners' was in Salisbury in the summer of 1945.

The establishment of the Order of Christian Witness at a conference in Kingsway on 16 November 1946 is part of post-war history. But it was the natural next stage following the setting up of the Kingsway Preachers and the London Christian Campaigners. Thus if one is looking for the lasting achievements of the West London Mission in the Second World War, then laying the foundations of the Order of Christian Witness, which has survived into the later 1980s, must surely be one of the most important.

12

The Post-War Years

– I –

8 May 1945 was VE day and Japan surrendered to the allies on 2 September that year. These capitulations ended six years of slaughter and devastation, but they did not usher in immediate prosperity. The British people experienced several years of austerity before wartime restrictions were raised. Bread rationing was introduced, after more than a year of peace, on 21 July 1946, and remained for two years. Nearly all clothing was still rationed three years after the war had ended and new furniture was available only to newly-weds or to those who had been bombed out of their homes. In many respects far more serious was the acute fuel shortage of the first quarter of 1947. On 23 January that year there began a six weeks' spell of icy weather, making it the most severe winter within living memory.[1] Drastic economies in the use of solid fuel, electricity and gas were enforced. At Hinde Street and Kingsway Hall Sunday evening congregations had difficulty in reading their hymn sheets as only half the lights were switched on. The children shivered in the crèche as supplies of coke were inadequate for the central heating system. The second-hand clothing department at 37 Grafton Way did a roaring trade.

The view of the incoming Labour government of 1945 under the premiership of Clement Attlee was that a substantial amount of government intervention was needed for both social planning and social justice. The nationalization of major industries including civil aviation (1946), coal (1947), transport and electricity (1948), gas (1949) and steel (1951) was considered as complementing reforms in the social services highlighted in the Family Allowances Act 1945 and the National Insurance, National Insurance (Industrial Injuries) and National Health Service Acts of 1946. These ushered in the Welfare State, broadly along the lines mapped out by Beveridge in his famous report of 1942.

Once Parliament had passed these measures, which were designed to ensure that all those experiencing the misfortune of unemployment, ill-health or injury were guaranteed enough income to meet their basic needs, as well as free medical treatment and hospitalization, it might be questioned whether there was still the necessity for the social work of the West London Mission. Hugh Price Hughes and his successors had shown where there was need and had gone some way to meet it by opening the crèche, the labour bureaux, the dispensaries and the labour yards. Now more comprehensive agencies, with greater resources at their command, were meeting many of these needs on a larger scale than could be provided by any private agency. However, the reforms of 1945–51 did not eliminate the problems of poverty, and some of the achievements of those six years of benevolent legislation were soon being undermined. Thus one of the basic principles of the National Health Service, described recently as 'perhaps the most beneficial reform ever enacted in England',[2] was abandoned when Britain's involvement in the Korean War of 1950–1 led to the introduction of prescription charges for medicines and spectacles.

In the 1950s the view was widely held that the heavier taxation of the rich which had taken place in the war, and the welfare benefits received by the less well off, had largely eliminated the problem of poverty. Professor Lionel Robbins of the London School of Economics wrote of a tax structure which 'relentlessly, year by year, is pushing us towards collectivism and propertyless uniformity'.[3] However, in the perspective of time, taxation is seen to have only the most marginal influence on the distribution of wealth. Twenty years after Robbins's cry of alarm, Professor Halsey found 'quite spectacular inequalities' surviving, as shown by the fact that the richest one per cent of the population took home about the same amount as the poorest twenty per cent.[4] There was little redistribution through welfare payments, since these were largely self-financing by the contributors.

That there was still a long way to go before poverty was eliminated, and therefore still scope for the relief and rescue work of the Mission, was revealed by the fact that in 1977, when the national unemployment rate was only 5.5% (compared with

13.5% in 1985), no less than 4,750,000 persons were in receipt of supplementary benefit.[5]

Nevertheless there was a remarkable rise in the standard of living of millions of people in the third quarter of the present century. The ownership of 'wealth for use' in the form of radios, televisions, washing machines and motor cars spread impressively. (At the same time, what Professor R. H. Tawney described as 'wealth for power', i.e. property which carries with it control over the lives of people, was still heavily concentrated in a few hands.)[6] By 1961 vacuum cleaners were to be found in three-quarters of British homes, while one in every three homes had a refrigerator and four out of every five boasted a TV set. When petrol rationing was abolished in May 1950 there were 2.3 million private cars on British roads. Ten years later the number had shot up to 5.6 million and by 1982 it was over 16 million. The bonanza in the purchase of consumer durables was encouraged by the colour supplements of the Sunday newspapers, led by *The Sunday Times*, which issued its first colour supplement in 1962. These lavish productions were financed by dozens of full page advertisements in which many of the seven deadly sins, but particularly pride, envy, gluttony and avarice, were exploited to the full!

These developments presented new challenges to the Christian churches. The possession of a car could facilitate attendance at a place of worship; it also offered the alternative of a drive into the countryside or a weekend spent in the Cotswolds. More and more of those who worked in London were, through the possession of a car, encouraged to live much further away from the city. This change in the life-style of many people is part of the explanation why in 1981 the population of Greater London was some two million below what it had been forty years earlier, though the loss of 683,000 industrial jobs in the 1960s and 1970s, a loss which was not fully offset by the growth of service employments, is also part of the explanation. Even in 1980 nearly half London households possessed no motor car. For members of these families bus services became less frequent and more expensive as London Transport endeavoured to cut its costs to offset the declining revenue which resulted from increased car usage. The availability of television in the home encouraged people to sit in comfort in their armchairs rather than making the effort of travelling to church.

A more serious challenge to the Christian church was the spread of the permissive society, which went hand in hand with the growth of a market economy. Parliament made it easier to get a divorce, lay a bet, or publish pornographic literature. One author described changes in the BBC as follows: 'Auntie BBC didn't just hitch up her skirt, she took it off altogether.'[7] In earlier decades decisions on public policy or private behaviour had often been taken on moralist grounds. A projected action was declared to be either 'right' or 'wrong'. Increasingly in the post-war decades 'moralism' gave place to 'casualism', which involved a weighing up of the pros and cons of a course of action to discover which decision on balance had least practical disadvantages. In the arts there was a retreat from the sugary and sentimental plays and films of the 1940s to the violent and sadistic productions of the 1970s.

– II –

In the light of the evacuation of many business firms and virtually all the higher education establishments from central London and the dangers from air raids and the black out, church membership at Kingsway was well maintained during the Second World War when more than 500 persons 'were on the books'. These high numbers were sustained into the early 1960s. Thereafter, with the shift of population to the outer suburbs and the rising costs of public transport, a gradual decline set in. By 1967 the membership figure was down to just under 400. Six years later it had dropped below the 300 mark.[8]

However, for at least two decades after the war the church was flourishing. In March 1947 sixty new members attended the service of recognition, and in the following month the numbers attending the Sunday evening services were 'the best since 1939'.[9] The 'power house' of the church was the Tuesday evening Guild Meeting (formerly meeting on Thursdays), at this time frequently attended by over 100 persons. After hymns, prayer and a short address by Donald Soper the class groups met separately for Bible study and free-ranging discussion. At the Wednesday morning staff meeting the leaders of the various social work projects reported on the past week's developments and planned future activities. The Community Centre in Wesley House was at the heart of many of the Mission's activities. The Luncheon Club provided meals to members of the Kingsway staff and to those who joined the club from nearby offices; Guild members met there for refreshments and discussion from 5.30 to 6.45 on Tuesday evenings. Refreshments were again served before and after Sunday evening services. On the first and third Sunday evenings of the month there would be hymn-singing; on the second Sunday there was an 'Open Forum' addressed by prominent speakers on such diverse subjects as disarmament, the Middle East crisis, or the emergence of new African states. A musical recital was given on the fourth Sunday. That the catering side of the Community Centre activities went smoothly was largely due to the unstinted services of Olive Delves and Ethel Kent over many years.

The Order of Christian Witness, whose origins were described in the previous chapter, grew from strength to strength in the early post-war years. Dozens of campaigns were conducted in many parts of the country. At Elland, for example, in November 1947, ten campaigners conducted eleven services and at the final rally no less than 120 persons took the Pledge of the Order to be a witness for Christ in a community of believers.[10]

Through the post-war era the meetings in Hyde Park and on Tower Hill were continued and until the 1980s they generally attracted large audiences, some members of which subsequently attended Kingsway services and joined in the life of the church. The heckling was generally good-humoured; but on 11 January 1948 Donald Soper had 'the worst meeting he had ever known in the Park' when an attempt was made to get hold of the stand. It appears that those responsible were members of the Communist Party of Great Britain who had been denied the opportunity of hiring a room for a meeting at Kingsway.[11]

The principal new development in the Mission's social work in the first years of peace was running the Hungerford Club, renamed simply 'The Hungerford' in January 1946. The move of the former shelterers and the staff from the Charing Cross arches took place on 26 February 1946, transport being provided by the Westminster City Council.[12] The old Lambeth Workhouse casual ward at 25a Wincott Street needed 'revolutionary treatment' before it was considered suitable for its new use. This treatment was provided by twenty-two volunteers from Kingsway who cleaned and redecor-ated the premises in the week preceding the move.[13] Numbers accommodated gradually increased. In December 1946 it was sixty per night. A year later it was sixty-five, of whom twenty were women. By 1950 average attendance was up to 90. The residents, who had the one common characteristic of homelessness, were sent by various organizations: the police; the Labour Exchange; the National Assistance Board; Welfare Officers; Mental After-care Committees and hospital almoners. In November 1950 a BBC radio appeal brought in £1,360 18s. 5d., but the balance of the cost of running the hostel that year, which was £744, was met out of Mission funds. The residents were provided with three meals a day at a total cost of 2s.[14] On 2 July 1948 forty-four residents were taken by coach for a day's outing by the Sussex seaside; for a number of them it provided not only their first sight of the sea but also their first ride in a coach.[15]

In the more than forty years since the end of the Second World War the members of the West London Mission have sought to follow John Wesley's advice that Methodists should not merely go to those who wanted them but to those who wanted them most. In pursuit of this policy it has sometimes been deemed wise to close some hostels where the need for them became less urgent and to open others as new emergencies arose in society.

Two activities which continued for a longer span of time than any others were the crèche and the second-hand goods (mainly clothes) depot. The babies and young children of working mothers were cared for in the crèche on the sixth floor at Kingsway until the building finally passed out of the hands of the Mission in 1980. It was a ninety-two year long record of service unsurpassed in this field. As the flow diagram in Appendix I reveals, the second-hand clothes depot eventually closed at 84 Caledonian Road in 1977, having occupied three different sites since the war. There were times in the later 1940s when a great deal of useful business was done. In 1947, for example, over 15,000 people visited the depot, and receipts from the sale of clothes, often at merely nominal prices, amounted to between £90 and £100 a week.[16] Thirty years later, however, the case for keeping the store open was weaker as other organizations, most notably Oxfam, were now meeting the need.

Although the population of Greater London as a whole was declining in the second half of the century, employment of young people, and especially young women, in retail trade and the social services was increasing. To provide accommodation for girls and young women between the ages of seventeen and twenty who 'were trying desperately to be self supporting and to take their rightful place in society' a new hostel was opened at Siddons Buildings, Drury Lane, in the autumn of 1948 and given the name of Gertrude Owen House in memory of Sister Gertrude who died on 13 March that year, after giving a lifetime of service to the Mission, most notably in managing the Sister Mabel Hostel between the wars. The new hostel filled the gap left by the closure of Emerson Bainbridge House at Kingsway in 1945. In 1951 the location of Gertrude Owen House was changed to 15 Highbury New Park, where it remained for the rest of the decade. Young people of both sexes were cared for at a restored Emerson Bainbridge House at 47 Cleveland Street (following war damage) in 1947. This remained open for twenty-one years. There was also Fellowship House at 25–26 Norland Square which provided a home for young people between 1947 and 1971.

Another development in the post-war world was the rapid increase in the number of unmarried mothers, many of whom were ostracized and some of whom were disowned by their families. To meet this growing need Kingsway House, a home for sixteen unmarried mothers and their babies, was opened at 28 Highbury Grove in 1951. This community, in which 'each mother was given the very best opportunity to be as independent, as imaginative and as responsible as possible in the management of her child',[17] stayed open until 1958 when it was decided to allocate the hostel to the more urgent need of caring for young offenders. Five years later, in 1963, the work with unmarried mothers was revived at Hopedene, 15 Aubert Park, and continued there for twenty-two years, though residential work was discontinued in July 1984. In 1985 an Independent Highbury Nursery was formed to continue the work in the building purchased from the West London Mission.

The Committee on Children and Young Persons, reporting in 1960, pointed to 'a tremendous material, social and moral revolution' over the preceding decades. Although in some ways life was more secure, the future seemed never more uncertain with nuclear weapons threatening to obliterate life on much of the planet. The material revolution, on the other hand, provided more desirable objects, greater opportunity for acquiring them illegally, and considerable chances of immunity from the consequences of so doing.[18]

This, together with a new aggressiveness and hostility to authority among growing numbers of young people, goes some way to explain the increase in indictable offences, particularly among the under twenty-fives. It was to meet these new challenges that Katherine Price Hughes House was established at 8 Doughty Street in 1937 and, twenty years later, moved to more suitable premises at 28 Highbury Grove. The hostel held up to twenty-two residents. For three decades (for most of which time it was given the financial backing of the Home Office) it was managed by the highly capable Sheila Townson, who never hesitated to speak her mind to the Superintendent. In October 1948 she reported that her girls objected to compulsory attendance at Sunday morning worship and that there had been 'a minor riot' on this issue. At her suggestion, backed by senior probation officers, a requirement to attend worship at Kingsway Hall was added to the conditions of admission to the hostel. She also questioned the use of the word 'rescue': her girls claimed that they did not need 'rescuing'. Donald Soper saw her point, but said that until a better word was suggested, 'rescue' would have to serve.[19]

According to a recent publication of the Office of Health Economics, 'Britain as it entered the post-war world was probably as "sober" a country as it has ever been in recorded history'.[20] Twenty years later this was certainly no longer the case. A huge expansion in overseas travel resulted in British drinking habits becoming more 'continental' in character, with wine and spirit drinking challenging the long supremacy of beer as the national drink; full employment, with extra earnings from overtime payments, coincided in time with the slower rise in alcohol prices than the rise in the price of food; the relative affluence of teenagers resulted in drunkenness spreading to people in much younger age groups; a degree of emancipation of women helped the removal of restraints on female drinking; supermarket chains were opened where the purchase of alcoholic drinks was made 'respectable' and the expenditure on alcohol advertising was twenty times as great as that on public warnings of the dangers of alcohol abuse. All these factors played a part in giving Britain a serious 'drink problem' by the 1960s.

This was the situation which persuaded Donald Soper in 1961 to change the use of the Hungerford hostel, which was converted to a rehabilitation centre for men and women suffering from alcoholism; it changed its name to St Luke's and St Mary's. The new centre was staffed by well-qualified nurses and social workers under the leadership of an experienced Warden/Project Director. Candidates for admission have been first treated (if necessary) in the detoxification unit and then after careful assessment have either been referred elsewhere or admitted as residents. Initially most residents were in employment outside the hostel; but by the 1980s, with a serious rise in the number of jobless, even in the London area, the majority were without paid employment. Some of the hostel residents, after a period of sobriety, were able to rejoin their families. For others, 'second stage' houses were established at Stirling Court and Argyll House in Clapham Road in 1967, where 'bed sits' with cooking facilities were provided so that each resident can have privacy, but also the support and friendship of one another and of a resident warden. A further development occurred in 1977, when Grove House, Bolingbroke Grove was made available for use as flats for ex-residents of St Luke's after it had been for five years a hostel for young ex-offenders. Through the generous co-operation of the Lambeth Mission, which placed its large hall at the disposal of the project leader of St Luke's, a Walk-in Centre, open in the afternoon from Monday to Friday for tea and sandwiches, recreational facilities, and, above all, information and help, was opened in July 1985 for those with alcohol and other problems. Though the official title of the rehabilitation centre has always been St Luke's and St Mary's, the treatment there of women sufferers from alcoholism has gone largely by default. It is thought that although at least one-third of the half million or so persons who are victims of alcohol abuse in Britain are women, at no time were there more than three women residents at the Wincott Street centre. It proved extremely difficult for the staff to secure the admission of more than one or two women at a time and then the handful of women who were admitted found living in a hostel dominated by, say, thirty-five male residents extremely difficult. Nevertheless, St Luke's looks set to becoming one of the longest surviving and most valuable pioneering undertakings of the West London Mission.

Alfred Hartley House at 1–5 Siddons Buildings, Drury Lane,

opened as a home for the elderly in 1953, was named after a man who gave great service to the Mission as its treasurer. Since it was only just 'round the corner' from Kingsway Hall, it was certainly convenient for members of the church who were not so mobile as they once had been. An additional home for the elderly was opened at Goodliffe House, 28 Sydenham Hill, in 1958. After the Mission had moved its headquarters to Hinde Street in 1980 both these houses were closed, after much heart-searching, the Drury Lane premises being converted to flats by the local authority in 1981 and Goodliffe House following in 1986. The Division of Social Responsibility of the Methodist Church had always considered these two projects to be out on a limb compared with the other undertakings of the Mission, since it was felt that the nationally organized Homes for the Aged were available to meet the need.

As the official figure of the number of homeless households in England (as measured under the inadequate definition provided under the Housing [Homeless Persons] Act of 1977) rose sharply from 53,000 in 1978 to 83,000 in 1984, and more and more single homeless people were to be seen sheltering for the night in cardboard boxes on London's pavements, the case for providing some relief and comfort for such people became more pressing.[21] When the Hungerford had been closed in 1961 the need had not been so great, but now it was manifestly urgent. Hence the Day Centre was opened in the spacious basement area of Kingsway Hall in 1973. Here there was an opportunity for recreation, warmth and refreshment, and just before Kingsway passed out of the control of the Mission the Centre was transferred to 136 Seymour Place, nearer the Hinde Street Church.

Some of the workers who were familiar with the activities of the Day Centre felt that a gesture should be made to help the homeless and lonely for at least one evening a week. This was the origin of the Wednesday Club, which began to meet regularly in 1975. At first the meeting place was the Community Centre at Kingsway. When this closed, temporary accommodation was found in a basement room lent by Holy Trinity Church, Kingsway, until a more permanent home was found on the Hinde Street premises at the beginning of 1986.

The record of the post-war years at Kingsway when Donald Soper was Superintendent of the West London Mission would be incomplete without reference to the gospel which he seized every opportunity to proclaim, whether the occasion was some church anniversary, a BBC programme, such as 'Any Questions', or a series of lectures at Yale University in the USA.[22] Over twenty years ago he declared, in a BBC 'Frankly Speaking' programme, that in his judgment 'it was not possible to be a practising Christian . . . without having a clear idea as to how Christianity is politically interpreted'.[23] This view was completely in the tradition of his two most distinguished predecessors as Superintendent: Hugh Price Hughes and J. Ernest Rattenbury. That it is a continuing tradition in the Christian Church was illustrated recently by Bishop Desmond Tutu of Johannesburg who said, 'I am puzzled about which Bible people are reading when they suggest religion and politics don't mix'.[24] The two pillars of the social gospel that Donald Soper proclaimed were pacifism and Christian Socialism. His pacifism sprang from the non-violent example of Jesus leading to his death on the cross. His Christian Socialism was derived from the reports, at the end of Chapters 2 and 4 of Acts, on how the first Christians behaved: 'They had all things in common.' In 1960 he was one of the signatories of *Papers from the Lamb*, the publication of which marked the launching of the Christian Socialist Movement.

– III –

The drop in membership at Hinde Street during the Second World War was severe. Many of those who had worked in London were evacuated or left for the suburbs at the weekend for the understandable reason of wishing to avoid air raids. The figures of membership fell from 178 in 1939 to 145 in 1942 and 107 in 1947.

When the Methodist students of Bedford College (University of London) were in 'exile' in Cambridge during the war years they linked up with the members of the Cambridge University Methodist Society. On their return to the capital in 1944 they decided that it would be a good idea to try to establish a University of London Methodist Society and they looked for a church to make their home. At this point Donald Soper could have made out a good case for them to come to Kingsway Hall, which at that time was the Mecca of young people (including students) of radical views. Instead he held his hand, knowing that both membership and church attendance at Hinde Street were very low at the time. The London Mission district officers advised the Bedford College students to go to Hinde

Street, where they would be very welcome. When twelve students took this advice on the first Sunday in October 1944 they found they were doubling the size of the congregation! They also noticed that it was the practice of the church stewards to rope off the side aisles before the start of the evening service so that the congregation would concentrate in the centre pews and not appear so disconsolately dispersed throughout the church. When the Revd E. R. Richardson took over as minister in September 1947 and saw the ropes being placed across the side pews, he exploded. He called it 'an insult to the Holy Spirit'. 'One day it will be full,' he said. It was a prophecy which was not fulfilled during his time at Hinde Street.

However, thanks to the growth of student numbers in London and the energetic efforts of successive ministers and of Miss Alice Walton, the number of students attending the church rose dramatically – the Revd Arnold Cooper wrote thirty years later of a seemingly 'unbelievable' growth in numbers – so that by the mid-1950s some 250–350 were coming to the Sunday evening services. They were organized into over twenty class groups for weekday and Sunday discussions, and they all met together for what was affectionately known as 'Methsoc' on the Sunday afternoons at 4.00 p.m. In the course of the University year thirty meetings were held, and a printed card programme listing the distinguished speakers who were to lead the discussion was circulated. The group leaders for each week met the chaplain at 2.30 on the Sunday afternoon for what was called a 'pilot group' discussion or briefing in preparation for the main meeting.

At the same time as student numbers were increasing, professional and service employment was growing, and many of those newly employed decided to set up home within the London boroughs rather than the outer suburbs. This was the basis for the expansion of Hinde Street membership, which rose alongside the growth of Methsoc. By 1962 a peak post-war church membership of 361 was reached. It was a caring community. No social welfare schemes were sponsored such as those which were managed from Kingsway, but contact was established with the Marylebone Borough Council, who informed church 'activists' of individual cases of loneliness, neglect and poverty. These people would be visited by John Hicks and others who arranged teams to spring-clean and redecorate homes between Friday afternoon and Sunday evening while temporary accommodation was provided for the residents over the weekend. Special consideration was given to newcomers to London, especially if they came from overseas. In case they were searching for somewhere to live in a transition period, the church was able to offer them accommodation at 178 Sutherland Avenue in West London, known, somewhat disrespectfully, by its occupants – and others – as the 'hindquarters'.

Some of the younger members of the church who had been members of 'Methsoc' established a Sunday Night Group which met after the evening service and had some similarity with the Kingsway Forum in that speakers were invited to lead discussions on the great issues of the day.

By the later 1950s the minister at Hinde Street had a very heavy work-load. In addition to the pastoral care of some 300 church members he had oversight of the Methodist work in the London colleges, and was Free Church Chaplain to the Middlesex Hospital and Medical School; he supervised the Nurses Fellowship and ran his own devotional class which was held in the Manse at 19 Thayer Street. That the church life was growing from strength to strength was revealed by what happened at the first Sunday evening service in October 1958. Shortly before the start, the church steward came through to the vestry to report that every seat in the main church was occupied and more people were seeking admission. What should he do? He was directed to lead people to the gallery, where spare hymn sheets were placed on the seats to cover the dust. Later that week a party of volunteers carried out some emergency cleaning. The gallery was regularly used for Sunday evening services in term time for some years after this.

It was this accession of strength which was one reason for the separation of the Hinde Street and Kingsway circuits in 1959. It was also considered that the church required an assistant minister, and that the likelihood of securing one would be enhanced if the separation took place and the request came from the Hinde Street Quarterly meeting. Moreover, in the words of Arnold Cooper, the minister at the time, Hinde Street 'had developed an ethos very different from that of Kingsway'. The Chairman of the North West London District, the Revd Lawrence C. Brooker, and the Secretary of the London Mission, Dr Ivonwy Morgan, were both sympathetic to the change. In 1962 the additional minister was secured. When the Revd Neville Ward succeeded the Revd Arnold Cooper in September he had the Revd Philip Rigby to assist him.

At both Kingsway Hall and Hinde Street through the second half of this century strong support was given to the ecumenical movement. Hinde Street joined a local Council of Churches in 1959 and an exchange of pulpits took place with other church members of the council. On Sunday 19 January 1969 Cardinal Archbishop Heenan, head of the Roman Catholic Church in England, preached at Hinde Street church. It was the first time that he had addressed the members of a Methodist church in his diocese. Although he stressed the dangers that lay ahead in any progress towards church unity and warned that some within his own church were 'less than enthusiastic', he conceded that the work of unity 'had begun and was of immense value'.[25] From September 1971 the Hinde Street church assumed responsibility for St Barnabas Anglican/Methodist church in Kensington which had recently been designated 'an area of ecumenical experiment' and was allocated a Methodist probationer minister. Donald Soper was throughout the post-war period a keen advocate of closer church unity. Links with Holy Trinity, the Anglican church in Kingsway, were built up in the 1970s. For a time the arrangement was that the Kingsway congregation would attend Sunday evening service at Holy Trinity once a month, while the Holy Trinity congregation would reciprocate on another Sunday. Later on, the Kingsway Sunday morning services were held at Kingsway and all Sunday evening services were at Holy Trinity.

Both Kingsway and Hinde Street ministers and congregations attached special importance to spiritual renewal. At Kingsway the year began with a week of 'internal mission' when there would be services every working day in the evening in order to meet the needs of those who might not be able to gt away for a weekend or could not manage a particular weekday evening. The week-end retreats conducted once a year from Hinde Street by the Revd Neville Ward were keenly appreciated and remembered. His successor, the Revd Brian Duckworth, introduced the concept of 'New Life on Sundays', when a major theme would be emphasized for the day and an attempt was made to bring the morning and evening congregations together by providing lunches and teas in the hope that those normally attending in the morning would stay on longer and those who normally came in the evening might turn up earlier! With any luck some of their times would overlap and the community life of the church would be strengthened.

— IV —

Sunday evening services at Kingsway normally started at 6.30 and ended at 7.45. However, on one Sunday early in 1971 the services ended promptly at 7.30 to enable some members to attend the meeting of the Parochial Church Council in Holy Trinity Church just up the road. Soon after the congregation had moved from the main hall to the crush hall a long drawn-out noise, like a roll of thunder, was heard. It was soon discovered that a large section of the main roof of the hall had collapsed. Mercifully the hall was empty and nobody was killed or even injured; but there certainly would have been severe injuries and possibly deaths if the service had continued as usual until 7.45, since large steel girders fell on to seats which a few minutes earlier had been occupied by worshippers.[26]

This catastrophe brought to a head the whole question of the Kingsway Hall building. The organ and choir area was found to be safe enough for continued use for orchestral rehearsals and recordings; but the cost of repairing other parts of the hall would have been very high. A further consideration was the fact that, in common with other 'Central Halls' of the Methodist Church, congregations were shrinking. When the great mission halls were established in the late-Victorian and Edwardian days of the popular music halls it was considered that members of the general public might not enter a church with pews but might be persuaded to enter a large hall with tip-up seats. However, by the 1970s the large halls were losing their appeal as places of worship. A decisive consideration was that if Kingsway Hall were sold the manifold social projects of the Mission could be sustained. Without the proceeds of the sale, their continuation was more problematic. The decision to sell off Kingsway Hall for £2½ million in 1975 was in line with the disposal of other large Central Halls including the Albert Hall, Manchester; Eastbrook, Bradford and Bristol Central Halls. The Albert Hall, Nottingham, which J. E. Rattenbury did so much to establish and fill with worshippers, was closed in 1986.

In the case of Kingsway Hall that part of the complex of buildings known as Wesley House was leased back from the Clarendon Property Co. Ltd for ten years from 24 June 1975 for a rent of

£35,000 a year to 29 August 1980, when it was agreed that there would be a rent review.

At the Methodist Conference held in Harrogate in the early summer of 1971, Brian Duckworth, who was then in charge of the Hinde Street Circuit, talked over with Donald Soper the future relationships between the two churches.[27] They agreed, in broad principle, that a merger would be in the long-run interest of both. On 8 July 1971 Brian Duckworth wrote to Donald Soper summarizing the approaches to the projected merger from the Kingsway and Hinde Street points of view. Donald Soper's main concerns were to ensure the future of the West London Mission's social work and to retain a base for the Kingsway congregation so that his pastoral and spiritual work could continue. The Hinde Street trustees were mainly concerned with the redevelopment of their church site. A group with representatives from both churches was then appointed to draft a plan for the merger. On 21 February 1972 their report was endorsed by a special joint Quarterly Meeting of the two circuits, and on the proposal of Lord Soper, seconded by the Revd B. Duckworth, it was agreed unanimously to make application to the Methodist Conference of 1972 for the circuits to be amalgamated. The Conference agreed to the proposal, which came into effect on 1 September that year.

One of the key recommendations of the report adopted by the joint Quarterly Meeting was that 'one of the first tasks of the united circuit should be to plan for the redevelopment of the Hinde Street site as a circuit venture'. In January and February 1973 the two churches' trusts appointed a joint working party to investigate the possibility of the redevelopment of the Hinde Street site. Feasibility studies were conducted in 1975, architects' plans drafted and approved in 1977. There were then considerable delays over a planning appeal and over the purchase of the property at 39 Marylebone Lane. In 1980 the contract for the first phase of the work of redevelopment was signed. Phase two of the work was carried out between 1980 and 1982, after which a greatly improved basement area, hall and new offices at 19 Thayer Street were available for use. The cost came to nearly £800,000.

In the meantime, in 1978, when Donald Soper was seventy-five years old, the Revd Dr John Newton, Principal and Tutor in Church

History at Wesley College, Bristol, was appointed to succeed him as Superintendent of the West London Mission.

One of the most memorable events in the history of the Mission took place in Kingsway Hall on the evening of Sunday, 30 July 1978, when Donald Soper's forty-two years as Superintendent were recalled in gratitude in a service attended by over 1,000 men and women. In tributes to the man whose message of Christian salvation had been proclaimed in the Hall since 1936 the Revd Arthur Shaw declared that, 'No man since John Wesley had linked so effectively preaching in the field with the Lord's Table.' The Roman Catholic Bishop of Central London was present and also a number of Anglican clergymen. Lord Soper's political colleague, the Rt Hon Michael Foot MP, Leader of the House of Commons, brought greetings from the Labour Party and from Socialists throughout the world. It was a heart-warming occasion.[28]

John Newton was born at Grantham in Lincolnshire, but otherwise has little in common with the present Prime Minister. He took an honours degree in History at the University of London in 1952 and for the next three years undertook research at the Universities of Hull and London where his most distinguished teacher was the late Professor R. H. Tawney. The subject of his PhD at the University of London in 1956 was 'Puritanism in the Diocese of York, 1603–1640'. He then did two years of theological training at Wesley House, Cambridge, for the Theological Tripos. His first circuit preaching appointment was at Louth in his native Lincolnshire and it was while there that he married Rachel Giddings, daughter of the Revd Maurice W. Giddings and Mrs Hilda Giddings.

The choice of John Newton to work for the merging of Kingsway and Hinde Street congregations was a very appropriate one. In common with Donald Soper he has a ready wit and a keen sense of humour. When they met to make arrangements for the transition in the Superintendency the following conversation took place:

Soper: Have you any children?

Newton: Yes, four boys. The youngest is two and the eldest fourteen.

Soper: Well, we had four girls. What a pity. If they were a bit younger and yours were a bit older I could have done business with you.

The transition to Hinde Street worked smoothly because it was a team effort. Donald Soper still had an important part to play in conducting a 10 o'clock Sunday morning communion service, in continuing the open air meetings at Tower Hill and Hyde Park, and in broadcasting. The Revd John Richardson helped to welcome the sometimes sensitive and critical former Kingsway members through his real concern for persons and his lively, cheerful manner. His help was decisive in 1980–81 when he was in charge during John Newton's year as President of the Conference. Services at Kingsway came to an end in August 1980, after which most of the congregation joined the Hinde Street church.

The social work formerly directed from Kingsway was now a greatly added responsibility for the ministers at Hinde Street. Nevertheless, in some areas the work was extended, as when through the helpful co-operation of the Revd Michael Fielding of the Lambeth Mission, the 'Walk-in' advice centre for those with alcohol and other problems was opened as an extension of the work of the St Luke's Rehabilitation Centre, and when in 1986 The Bridge project for young people in need of care was opened in the refurbished Emerson Bainbridge House at 335 Clapham Road. When it is remembered that for at least half the century-long history of the Mission the Sisters played a large part in the running of the social work projects, the work load placed on John Newton and his assistant the Revd Ken Howcroft can well be imagined.

Despite the heavy responsibilities of active church members who serve on the House Committees of the social work projects and on the committees of the church, recent years have seen a welcome revival of the musical, dramatic and artistic activities of the Mission church. In collaboration with the London Baroque Opera Group, Molière's *Le Malade Imaginaire* had been produced. Among the plays recently produced have been *Larkrise* by Keith Dewhurst; *Wesley* by Howard Benton; *The Roses of Eyam* by Don Taylor; *Riders to the Sea* by J. M. Synge and *Black Comedy* by Peter Shaffer.

The international links established by the Kingsway and Hinde Street churches have been extensive and invaluable. These have come into being partly through visitors from overseas countries joining the church services and partly through the ministers having served abroad in the course of their careers, as did John Newton in

Kenya, John Richardson in Korea and Stuart Jordan in Argentina. In 1953 when Donald Soper was President of the Methodist Conference, he and Mrs Soper paid a visit to the churches in Antigua. They were appalled to find, within a stone's throw of the hotel in which they were staying, people being left to die in ditches by the side of the street. When they returned to England the congregation at Kingsway organized a series of Saturday evening 'Antigua Parties' which raised money to build bungalows for the homeless on the island. The best known former worshipper at Kingsway Hall is David Lange, currently the Prime Minister of New Zealand, who in a BBC television interview with Donald Soper early in 1986 emphasized how much he had been influenced in the direction of Christian Socialism and pacifism when he was resident in England and attended the meetings in Hyde Park and on Tower Hill as well as the services in Kingsway Hall. In July 1962 the Ghanaian High Commissioner in London, Kwesi Armah, read the lesson at a special service organized by the Revd Arnold Cooper at Hinde Street to mark the second anniversary of Ghana's Republic Day. The High Commissioner subsequently wrote: 'Your kindness and co-operation with the Ghanaian community in diversified ways will for ever carry happy memories.'

Both Kingsway Hall and Hinde Street endeavoured to work for peace in a divided world by maintaining links with both the USA and with the countries of the Eastern bloc. The latest development in this continuing endeavour has been in association with the Methodist Kreuzkirche in Leipzig in the German Democratic Republic. Following a talk by Canon Edward Charles on the churches in Eastern Europe during 'One World Week' in October 1982, the idea was mooted of 'twinning' with a local church in Eastern Europe. Advice was taken from Methodist contacts, particularly from the Revd Peter Stephens of the European Affairs Committee, and the upshot was a favourable response from Pastor Wolfgang Maneck of the Leipzig Kreuzkirche. The Revd Stuart Jordan, the Students' Chaplain at Hinde Street, took a party of young people from the church to stay with families of the Leipzig church in the summer of 1985. In July 1986 a further week's visit was made and contacts were re-established. On that occasion Stuart Jordan preached a sermon in German in the Leipzig church. Individual members of the Kreuzkirche have visited Hinde Street and it is hoped that a group of members from that congregation will be able to attend the centenary celebrations of the West London Mission.

The international links of the Mission will be strengthened through the decision of the Methodist Conference to appoint the Revd Leslie J. Griffiths as Superintendent from September 1986. Henceforward not even the Superintendent will be English! Leslie Griffiths was born at Burry Port, Carmarthenshire, in 1942. After graduating with a BA degree in Mediaeval English at Cardiff and obtaining his Theological Tripos at Wesley College, Cambridge in 1969, he served for several years with churches in Haiti, including, during his final years there, superintending the Cap Haitian circuit.

13

Conclusions

In his *First Annual Report* of the West London Mission (called at that time the West Central Mission), Hugh Price Hughes quoted with obvious approval the words of William Arthur in *The Tongue of Fire* (1854) that 'nothing short of the general renewal of society ought to satisfy any soldier of Christ'. He had not always taken this standpoint. When he first met his future wife, Katherine, he held a somewhat complacent view of the society of his day. He came to accept Arthur's view following his reading of the startling exposures of slum conditions in Andrew Mearns' *Bitter Cry of Outcast London* and having become aware at first hand of the appalling living conditions of many Londoners. In the West End the poverty was doubly obscene in so far as it was immediately juxtaposed to flamboyant and excessive wealth. In his *Second Annual Report* he wrote of 'extreme contrasts of social misery and social merriment' in London's West End.

Hugh Price Hughes's primary aim, and that of his successors, was to spread the good news of the transformed life that was possible for those who followed the example and teaching of Jesus Christ. However, more than two years before he preached the first sermon he delivered in St James's Hall, he wrote in the newspaper he founded:

It is impossible to deal effectually with the spiritual destitution of London unless you deal also with the physical and mental destitution.[1]

It is because he held this belief that the various social projects for the relief of poverty became an integral part of the work of the Mission.

The message of those who followed Hugh Price Hughes was developed from the foundations he had laid. J. E. Rattenbury felt even more strongly that personal salvation would have to be accompanied by a complete change in the basis of society.

> 'Give us this day our daily bread' – and in this city men and women in hundreds and thousands tell you they have to go to the devil to get their daily bread or they would never get it at all. That is what actually happens. I am not exaggerating or using strong language for the sake of it. It is simply the truth today that thousands in this city are driven by poverty to vice and crime . . . Jesus prayed 'Lead us not into temptation'. The modern economic system is always leading us into temptation. The conditions under which people work are a continual pressure on the soul. So I speak of the Lord's Prayer. It means the reconstruction, the recreation of our social order, in order that the whole community of men and women, the children of God, may have a reasonable opportunity of getting it answered.
>
> I want to ask you. How about the social order of today? Is it true that man is valued most? Do we understand what *real* wealth is? The real wealth of the nation is in its men and women, and in nothing else.[2]

'That is all very true,' it may be said, 'but it has little applicability to the present-day situation. We must look to the future and not dwell on the iniquities of late Victorian and Edwardian times.' Such thoughts would be reassuring if they reflected reality.

Unfortunately the situation in the 1980s has some basic characteristics in common with that of the 1880s. It is true that there is not now the level of absolute poverty that existed when Hugh Price Hughes conducted his Sunday afternoon 'Conferences'. But poverty is a relative concept. In the 1880s people were saying that life for the poor was better than it was in the 'Hungry Forties'. The moral objection to poverty is that it isolates and divides people and hinders the development of real community. In 1978 the Supplementary Benefits Commission gave this concept official verification:

> Poverty in urban industrial centres like Britain is a standard of living so low that it excludes and isolates people from the rest of the community. To keep out of poverty they must have an income which enables them to participate in the life of the community.[3]

The 'extreme contrasts' deplored by Hugh Price Hughes a hundred years ago are still to be found:

> The Urban Priority Areas lie at the centre of an unequal society, their poverty obscured by the busy shopping precincts of mass consumption, their bare subsistence of dole and supplementary benefit existing alongside material opulence.[4]

Far from it being the case that inequalities are being lessened, the situation is worsening. 'In the nation as a whole since the end of the post-war era the rich have got richer and the poor poorer.' The best-off fifth of British households increased their share of *post-tax* income between 1976 and 1982 from 37.9 per cent to 39.4 per cent while the bottom fifth slipped from 7.4 per cent to 6.9 per cent.[5] These changes have meant 'a growing inequality of life chances, income, housing, education, public services and the general level of civic amenity'.[6]

Eighty-five years ago, just before he became Superintendent of the West London Mission, W. Ensor Walters wrote:

> The housing problem is bound up with the land question and the final solution will only be found when that question is grappled with.[7]

In the 1980s the Christian community in Britain has denounced the system in South Africa whereby 85% of the population are condemned to live on 13% of the land, that meagre allocation being land of the poorest quality. And yet little is said of the situation in Britain itself where the top 13% of landowners own 91.3% of the land.[8] Because what Ensor Walters saw as the 'land question' has not been grappled with, 'the wealthy price land so highly that a family unit must spend nearly a third of its income to keep a roof over its head.'[9]

In 1889 Hugh Price Hughes wrote:

> The special pinch of poverty in West Central London is due to the fact that rent is so much higher than in other poor quarters . . . Hence a ten roomed house constantly contains ten families, all of them on the verge of starvation.[10]

Over ninety years later the people of the area were not 'on the verge of starvation', but the Census of Population in 1981 reported that the two boroughs of Westminster and Kensington and Chelsea had the worst overcrowding in London 'with over thirty per cent of households living in overcrowded conditions'.[11] The overcrowding had the same immediate cause as was present when Hugh Price Hughes wrote his Annual Report – rent was 'so much higher than in other poor quarters'.

– II –

As has been recorded in Chapter 7, when the West London Mission reached an important milestone in its history in entering into possession of Kingsway Hall not long before the outbreak of the First World War, J. E. Rattenbury used the occasion to prompt the Quarterly Meeting into a consideration of its objectives for the future. The celebration of a centenary provides just such another occasion. It is worth recalling Dr Rattenbury's words since they form as appropriate an introduction to finding the way forward in the closing years as they were for the early years of the twentieth century:

> We ought to find means of reaching spiritually all the different types and classes of people in the neighbourhood . . . We must find means of studying the social conditions of life and all the various problems of social morality, and to set ourselves to find out what is needed to better the conditions of life around us.[12]

David Sheppard has recently warned that

> Sometimes church organisations are still meeting a need which they were founded to deal with two generations ago, even though that need has long since been met by someone else.[13]

Hugh Price Hughes was aware of this danger when he reminded readers in his *First Annual Report* of John Wesley's advice that Christian agents should go 'not where they are wanted but where they are wanted most'.[14] The Mission will need to be at least as alert and flexible in its approach to social problems in the future as it has been in the past if this advice is to be followed. David Sheppard's words are again appropriate:

> We need to be the kind of church that serves people where they are. It is the style of life of the church community which will decide for many people whether they will join or not.[15]

'Serving people where they are' means both in their home localities and in their places of work. *Faith in the City* has reminded us of the plight of the majority of the homeless – apart from those who want to be free to wander – often single-parent families, who are desperately anxious to find somewhere to live. 'Well over 10,000 families a year are being placed by local authorities in temporary accommodation, often in dirty, overcrowded and unsafe bed and breakfast hotels.'[16] Hundreds of these families are eking out an existence within a short distance of the Hinde Street Church. But the homeless are only one group among many that exist in a society that gives money-getting a greater importance than service to one's fellow men and women. Church members who in their places of residence are active in tenants' associations and residence associations could take the lead in taking action with and on behalf of such outcast groups in society.

Historically the West London Mission has fulfilled a valuable rôle in pointing out important social needs and setting an example in meeting them – admittedly on a small scale, because of limited resources. Sometimes these projects paved the way to more comprehensive and adequate provision by central or local government, as in the provision of unemployment insurance and the provision of residential homes for the elderly. Sometimes the Mission's work has been a valuable supplement to the work of the local authority or central government. There is a current danger that government will attempt to push back to voluntary bodies some of the responsibilities it has hitherto shouldered. If this were to happen it would reverse the experience of the years before 1939 when the Superintendents of the Mission complemented the work of the social projects with demands for legislation to remedy social abuses and meet social needs. The attacks on the Judaeo-Christian tradition of social righteousness and on 'egalitarianism', and the attempt to make the poor scapegoats and to label public sector spending as a 'burden', need to be resisted.

The West London Mission had been blessed with Superintendents who saw the problems of their time in a broad perspective. While they sponsored important projects for ameliorating social abuses, they kept alive a vision of God's Kingdom here on earth. J. E. Rattenbury spoke of a 'city of righteousness and truth and beauty and joy' and urged his congregations 'to enlist in this great crusade'. In our own time the members of the Archbishop of Canterbury's Commission were wise to remind us that 'the inner city and the peripheral estates are creatures of the whole society, not simply of their inhabitants'.[16]

The Revd Barney Pityana, a black priest of the Church of England, warned of churches 'that seek to win concessions from oppressive systems instead of seeking to change those systems'.[17] The best tradition of the West London Mission has been both to win concessions and to seek to change the system.

It may be said that there have been occasions in the past when the Mission has adopted too paternalistic an approach to social problems. The hope for the future is that people in need both in the church and without its walls will join together in a 'grass roots' approach to solving the problems of their time.

When the Mission was founded in 1887 'many people were driven into Christianity by their sin'. But as J. E. Rattenbury once declared:

> The spirit of God does not only convict men of sin, but of righteousness. There are some people who are driven into Christianity by their sin, but there are others who are wooed into Christianity by the attractive personality of the Saviour and the righteousness of God.[18]

It is significant that the influence of the West London Mission was at its peak when in the unpropitious surroundings of the Lyceum Theatre pre-eminence was given to a vision of the righteousness of the Kingdom of God to be experienced here on earth.

Appendix

Flow Chart of the Activities of the
West London Mission

WEST LONDON MISSION 1887–1987

MAIN PREACHING CENTRES

→St James' Hall → Exeter Hall → Gt Queen St → Lyceum → Kingsway Hall → Hinde St - - -
1887–1905   1905–6   1906–8   1908–12   1912–80   1980–

HALLS AND CHAPELS

Wardour Hall → **Craven Hall** → **Gt Queen St Hall** → **Wesley House** → **Hinde St** - - -
1887–94   1894–1905   1906–10   Kingsway   1980–
      1911–80

Cleveland Hall
1889–1914

People's Hall,
Chalton St
1892–1929

Princes' Hall
1887–95

Hengler's Circus
1905–6

MISSION HEADQUARTERS

Lincoln House → **Wesley House** → **Hinde St** - - -
1888–1911   1911–82   1982–

SOCIAL WORK

Creche	**Lincoln House** →	**Craven Hall** →	**Lincoln House**	**Wesley House**‖ - - -
	60 Greek St	Fouberts Place	60 Greek St	Kingsway
	1888–95	1895–1907	1907–11	1911–80
Rescue Home for Girls in Need of Care & Supervision	**Winchester House** →	**Winchester House** →	**Winchester House**	→ **Winchester House** →
	Walthamstow	20 Manor Place	5 Eastbourne Ter.	23 Ampthill Sq
	1892–8	1898–9	1899–1913	1913–18
	Sister Mabel Hostel →	**Katherine Price Hughes House**		
	1-5 Siddons Blgs, Drury Lane	8 Doughty St		
	1921–38	1937–57		
Home for Dying	**St Luke's House**	**St Luke's House** →	**St Luke's House** →	**St Luke's House** ‖ - - -
	50 Osnaburgh St	13–14 Lawn Rd	14 Pembridge Sq	Hereford Rd
	1893–1901	1901–2	1902–23	1923–
Second Hand Goods Depot	160 Wardour St →	131 Wardour St →	52-4 Cleveland St →	51A Cleveland St →
	1893–5	1895–1906	1894–1917	1917–39
	37 Grafton Way →	12 Bowling Green Lane →	84 Caledonian Rd	
	1939–49	1950–62	1963–77	
Holiday & Convalescent Homes	**Wesley House**	**Hopedene Holiday Home**	**Langham Hotel**	
	Bisley	Barnet	Worthing	
	1890–98	1919–38	1956–64	
Men's Social Dept	56 Cleveland St			
	1906–14			
Working Girls Hostel	**Emerson Bainbridge Hostel** →	**Emerson Bainbridge House**	**Gertrude Owen House** →	**Gertrude Owen House**
	47 Cleveland St	Kingsway	1–5 Siddons Blgs, Drury Lane	15 Highbury New Park
	1911–41	1941	1948–51	1951–60

Young Peoples Hostels	**Emerson Bainbridge House** Kingsway 1941–45	**Emerson Bainbridge House** 47 Cleveland St 1947–68	**Fellowship House** 25–6 Norland Sq 1947–71	
Maternity Hospital	**Parkhurst** Parkhurst Rd 1922–39			
Unmarried Mother & Baby Homes	**Kingsway House** 28 Highbury Grove 1951–8	**Henry Carter House** Camden Sq 1953–4	**Hopedene** ‖ - - - 15 Aubert Park 1963–85	
Unmarried Expectant Mother Home	**Grove House** 1 Bolingbroke Grove 1960–72			
Young Ex-Offenders Hostel	**Men's Hostel** 1–5 Siddons Blgs, Drury Lane 1938–46	**Henry Carter House** Camden Sq 1952–3	**Emerson Bainbridge House** 335–7 Clapham Rd 1971–84	**Grove House** Bolingbroke Grove 1972–7
Men and Women on Probation and Bail	**Katherine Price Hughes House** - - - 28 Highbury Grove 1958–			
Single Homeless	**The Hungerford** → Arch 176, Hungerford Lane 1941–6	**The Hungerford** 25A Wincott St 1946–60	**Day Centre** → Kingsway 1973–79	**Day Centre** - - - 136 Seymour Place 1979–

Alcoholics Recovery

St Luke's House - - - 25A Wincott St 1961–   Second Stage **Stirling Court** - - - 343 Clapham Rd 1967–   Day Centre **Lambeth Mission** - - - 1 Lambeth Rd 1985–

St Mary's House - - - 25A Wincott St 1963–   **Argyll House** Clapham Rd 1967–77

Grove House - - - 1 Bolingbroke Grove 1977–

Young People in Need	**The Bridge** - - - 335–7 Clapham Rd 1986–	
Homes for the Elderly	**Alfred Hartley House** 1-5 Siddons Blgs, Drury Lane 1953–81	**Goodliffe House** 28 Sydenham Hill 1958–86
Nurses' Hostel	Culmstock Rd 1974–7	
Principal Home of the Sisters	**Katherine House** → 19 Montague St 1887–91	**Katherine House** 10 Fitzroy Sq 1891–1914

KEY

- - -   = project continuing
‖ - - - = project continuing but not under WLM control
→   = direct transfer of project between addresses

Select Bibliography

A. *Unpublished Records*

The records of the Hinde Street church are deposited with the Westminster City Archives Department as Accession 594 and are currently housed in the Marylebone Public Library, Marylebone Road, London, NW1.

The records of the West London Mission, the Great Queen Street Chapel and associated chapels in the West London area are deposited in the Greater London Record Office (reference number N/M) at Bowling Green Lane, off Farringdon Road, London, EC4.

Although the above typescripts and manuscripts are packaged in over 500 bundles, there are gaps in the series. However, they are indispensible for any serious study of Methodism in London over the past two hundred years.

B. *Secondary Works*

1. *London in the 1880s*

C. Booth (ed.), *Life and Labour of the People of London*, 17 vols, Williams and Norgate, London 1889–1902
W. Booth, *In Darkest England and the Way Out*, Salvation Army, London 1890
G. Steadman Jones, *Outcast London*, Penguin, Harmondsworth 1976
A. S. Wohl, Introduction to A. Mearns, *The Bitter Cry of Outcast London*, Leicester University Press 1970

2. *The Forward Movement*

D. W. Bebbington, *The Nonconformist Conscience: Chapel and Politics 1870–1914*, Allen and Unwin, London 1902
D. P. Hughes, *The Life of Hugh Price Hughes*, Hodder and Stoughton, London 1905
K. P. Hughes, *The Story of my Life*, Epworth Press, London 1945
K. S. Inglis, *Churches and the Working Class in Victorian England*, Routledge & Kegan Paul, London 1963
E. R. Taylor, *Methodism and Politics*, Cambridge University Press 1935

3. *The Early Years of the West London Mission*

G. V. Bennett and J. Walsh (eds.), *Modern English Church History*, Adam and Charles Black, London 1966

P. d'A. Jones, *The Christian Socialist Revival 1877–1914*, University Press, Princeton 1968

R. Mudie-Smith, *The Religious Life of London*, Hodder and Stoughton, London 1904

J. A. Robinson (ed.), *Hugh Price Hughes as We Knew Him*, Horace Marshall, London 1907

T. M. Taylor, *Portraits and Pictures*, Stenlake and Simpson, London 1893

G. Unwin and J. Telford, *Mark Guy Pearse*, Epworth Press, London 1930

4. *The Sisters of the People*

W. Bradfield, *The Life of the Revd Thomas Bowman Stephenson*, C. H. Kelly, London 1913

D. P. Hughes, *The Sisters of the People and their World*, Horace Marshall, London 1905

K. P. Hughes, *The Story of my Life*, Epworth Press, London 1945

E. Pethick-Lawrence, *My Part in a Changing World*, Gollancz, London 1938

5. *The Social Work of the Mission before 1914*

The fullest accounts are given in the *Annual Reports* of the West London Mission.

J. D. Hilton, *Marie Hilton: Her Life and Work, 1821–1896*, Ibister, London 1897

H. P. Hughes, *Social Christianity: Sermons*, Hodder and Stoughton, London 1890

J. E. Rattenbury, *Six Sermons on Social Subjects*, Robert Culley, London 1908

A. and E. Walters, *Sir John Bamford Slack*, H. Kelly, London 1910

6. *The Open Air Witness*

H. Latimer, *Sermons*, J. M. Dent, London 1906

D. O. Soper, *The Advocacy of the Gospel*, Hodder and Stoughton, London 1961

D. O. Soper, *Tower Hill:12.30*, Epworth Press, London 1963

J. Stacey, *John Wyclif and Reform*, Epworth Press, London 1964

C. E. Walters, *The Open Air Speakers Handbook*, C. H. Kelly, London 1914

7. *Years of Turmoil*

G. Dangerfield, *The Strange Death of Liberal England*, Constable, London 1936

M. Edwards, *Methodism and England*, Epworth Press, London 1943

H. McLeod, *Class and Religion in the Late Victorian City*, Croom Helm, London 1974

8. *The Mission in World War I*

H. Carter, *The Control of the Drink Trade*, Longman, London 1918
M. MacDonagh, *In London during the Great War*, Eyre and Spottiswoode, London 1935
A. Marwick, *The Deluge*, Penguin Books, Harmondsworth 1967
C. S. Peel, *How we lived then*, John Lane, London 1929

9. *Hinde Street*

Anon, *Hinde Street Methodist Church, London, 1810–1960*, London 1960
A. W. Baldwin, *The Macdonald Sisters*, Peter Davies, London 1960
N. Curnock, *Hinde Street Chapel, 1810–1910*, Robert Culley, London 1910
F. W. Macdonald, *As a Tale that is told*, Cassell, London 1919
J. Telford, *Two West-End Chapels*, Wesleyan Methodist Book Room, London 1886

10. *The Inter-War Years*

C. L. Mowat, *Britain between the Wars*, Methuen, London 1955
W. Purcell, *Portrait of Soper*, Mowbrays, London 1972
D. O. Soper, *Christian Politics*, Epworth Press, London 1977
J. Stevenson, *Social Conditions in Britain between the Wars*, Penguin Books, Harmondsworth 1977
W. Temple, *Christianity and Social Order*, Penguin Books, Harmondsworth 1942
D. Thompson, *Donald Soper: a Biography*, Denholm House Press, Nutfield 1971
G. Weightman and S. Humphries, *The Making of Modern London, 1914–1939*, Sidgwick and Jackson, London 1984

11. *The War Years 1939–45*

Archbishop's Commission on Evangelism, *Towards the Conversion of England*, Church Assembly, London 1945
V. Brittain, *England's Hour*, Macmillan, London 1941
A. Calder, *The People's War*, Panther Books, London 1971
W. Sansom, *Westminster in War*, Faber and Faber, London 1947
R. F. Wearmouth, *Social and Political Influence of Methodism in the Twentieth Century*, Epworth Press, London 1957

12. *The Post-War Years*

P. Gregg, *The Welfare State*, Harrap, London 1967
A. H. Halsey, *Change in British Society*, Oxford University Press 1978
D. Martin, *Sociological Yearbooks of Religion in Britain*, SCM Press, London 1968–

A. Marwick, *British Society since 1945*, Penguin Books, Harmondsworth 1982

D. O. Soper, *Calling for Action*, Robson Books, London 1984

13. *Conclusion*

Archbishop of Canterbury's Commission on Urban Priority Areas, *Faith in the City*, Church House Publishing, London 1985

S. G. Evans, *The Social Hope of the Christian Church*, Hodder and Stoughton, London 1965

J. J. Vincent, *OK Let's be Methodists*, Epworth Press, London 1984

Notes

1. London in the 1880s

1. M. Dessauer-Meinhardt, 'Monthly Unemployment Records 1854–1897', *Economica* New Series, Vol. VII (August 1940), pp. 322–6.
2. A. Marshall, 'The Housing of the London Poor: 1. Where to House them', *Contemporary Review* (February 1884), p. 226.
3. Cited in J. Harris, *Unemployment and Politics*, London 1973, p. 54.
4. K. D. Brown, *Labour and Unemployment*, Newton Abbot 1971, p. 14
5. B. Gilbert, *The Evolution of National Insurance in Great Britain*, London 1966, p. 28.
6. A. S. Wohl, Introduction to A. Mearns, *The Bitter Cry of Outcast London*, Leicester 1970, p. 16.
7. *Methodist Recorder*, 1 February 1884.
8. For examples see *Pall Mall Gazette*, 3 and 6 November and 12 December 1883.

2. The Forward Movement: Ferment within Methodism

1. *The Methodist Times*, 29 September 1887.
2. Katherine Price Hughes, *The Story of my Life*, London 1945, p. 43.
3. D. W. Bebbington, *The Noncomformist Conscience: Chapel and Politics 1870–1914*, London 1982, p. 40; D. P. Hughes, *The Life of Hugh Price Hughes*, London 1905, pp. 4, 10, 78, 85, 134.
4. K. P. Hughes, *Story*, p. 64; D. P. Hughes, *Life*, p. 167.
5. K. S. Inglis, *The Churches and the Working Classes in Victorian England*, London 1963, p. 70.
6. K. P. Hughes, *Story*, p. 64.
7. Bebbington, *Noncomformist Conscience*, p. 13.
8. *The Methodist Times*, 19 August 1886, p. 557.
9. E. R. Taylor, *Methodism and Politics*, Cambridge 1933, p. 211.
10. *Methodist Recorder*, 17 February 1898.
11. W. J. Townsend, H. B. Workman and G. Earys, *A New History of Methodism*, London 1909, Vol. 1, p. 456.
12. *Methodist Recorder*, 7 December 1883.
13. *The Methodist Times*, 12 March 1885.
14. *The Methodist Times*, 30 July 1885.
15. *Minutes of Conference*, July 1884, pp. 310, 281.
16. *Minutes of Conference*, July 1885, p. 228.
17. Ibid., p. 265.
18. *The Methodist Times*, 28 May 1886.
19. *The Methodist Times*, 18 February 1886.

20. *Methodist Recorder*, 23 July 1886.
21. *Methodist Recorder*, 23 July 1886.
22. *The Methodist Times*, 18 February 1886.
23. *The Methodist Times*, 29 July 1886.
24. *The Methodist Times*, 5 August 1886.
25. *The Methodist Times*, 17 May 1886.
26. *The Methodist Times*, 5 August 1886.

3. *The Early Years of the West London Mission*

1. The West Central Mission *First Annual Report*, 1888, p. 2. This was the only report to be attributed to the West *Central* Mission.
2. *Methodist Recorder*, leading article 'Methodism in London', 14 December 1883.
3. The West London Mission (hereafter referred to as WLM), *Second Annual Report*, 1889, p. 5.
4. G. Steadman Jones, *Outcast London*, Oxford 1971, p. 219.
5. P. Glass, *Hugh Price Hughes and the West London Mission*, Part II Theological and Religious Studies Tripos Dissertation, March 1985, Wesley House, Cambridge.
6. *The Methodist Times*, 4 November 1886.
7. *The Methodist Times*, 8 September 1887.
8. The West Central Mission *First Annual Report*, 1888, p. 3.
9. J. Armitage Robinson (ed.), *Hugh Price Hughes as We Knew Him*, London 1907, p. 24.
10. The West Central Mission, *First Annual Report*, 1888, p. 2.
11. T. Morcom Taylor, *Portraits and Pictures of the West London Mission*, London 1893, p. 6.
12. The West Central Mission, *First Annual Report*, 1888, p. 5.
13. Ibid., p. 10.
14. Taylor, *Portraits and Pictures*, p. 9.
15. P. Glass, *Hugh Price Hughes*, p. 12.
16. Taylor, *Portraits and Pictures*, p. 17.
17. O. Chadwick, *The Victorian Church*, Part 2, London 1972, p. 323.
18. Mark Guy Pearse, in Robinson, *Hugh Price Hughes*, p. 24.
19. C. Booth, *Life and Labour of the People of London*, Vol. 2, London 1902, p. 195.
20. The West Central Mission, *First Annual Report*, 1888, p. 5.
21. Taylor, *Portraits and Pictures*, p. 8.
22. The West Central Mission, *First Annual Report*, 1888, p. 8.
23. Ibid., pp. 10–12.
24. The above paragraph is based on the account in Taylor, *Portraits and Pictures*, pp. 19–23. The Revd T. Morcom Taylor was in charge of the Cleveland Hall centre from 1890–3.
25. WLM, *The Story of our Work*, 1896, pp. 53–9.
26. WLM, *Eighth Annual Report*, 1894, p. 5.
27. *Wesleyan Methodist Magazine*, February 1873.
28. R. Mudie-Smith, *The Religious Life of London*, London 1904, p. 7.
29. Peter d'A. Jones, *The Christian Socialist Revival 1877–1914*, Princeton 1968, p. 64.
30. Quoted in M. Edwards, *Methodism and England*, London 1943, p. 147.

31. Lady Henry Somerset in J. A. Robinson (ed.), *Hugh Price Hughes as we Knew Him*, pp. 19–20.

32. WLM, *Second Annual Report*, 1889, p. 17.

4. *The Sisters of the People*

1. O.Schreiner, *Women and Labour*, London 1911, p. 33.

2. Katherine Price Hughes, *The Story of my Life*, London 1945, p. 37.

3. Ibid., p. 67.

4. E. Pethick-Lawrence, *My Part in a Changing World*, London 1938, p. 72; Anon. 'Mrs Hughes: A Character Sketch', *The Young Woman*, No. 5, February 1893, p. 151.

5. W. Bradfield, *The Life of the Rev Thomas Bowman Stephenson*, London 1913, pp. 289–90; Mrs Katherine Price Hughes interviewed by Mr E. P. Bainbridge, in *West London Mission: The Story of our Work*, 1907, p. 26.

6. WLM, *Annual Report*, 1890, p. 7.

7. WLM, *Annual Report*, 1893, p. 19.

8. *WLM: The Story of our Work*, 1907, p. 30.

9. Hughes, *The Story of My Life*, p. 73; WLM, *Annual Report*, 1899, p. 23; *WLM: The Story of our Work*, 1907, p. 26.

10. This account of Emmeline Pethick-Lawrence is based on her autobiography, *My Part in a Changing World*.

11. M. Neal and F. Kidson, *English Folk Song and Dance*, London 1915.

12. *WLM: The Story of our Work*, 1907, p. 26.

13. *Advance* (the WLM magazine), October 1889, p. 6.

14. WLM, *Annual Report*, 1890, p. 20.

15. WLM, *Annual Report*, 1899, p. 32.

16. Sister Emmeline, 'The Life of a Sister of the People', *The Young Woman*, January 1894, p. 129.

17. Ibid.

18. Sister Lily, writing in *Advance*, December 1889.

19. WLM, *Annual Report*, 1889, pp. 66, 69.

20. WLM, *Annual Report*, 1890, p. 67.

21. WLM, *Annual Report*, 1891, p. 47.

22. Ibid.

23. WLM, *Annual Report*, p. 55.

24. WLM, *Annual Report*, 1895, pp. 24–8.

25. WLM, *Annual Report*, 1893, p. 19.

26. WLM, *Annual Report*, 1898, p. 29.

27. WLM, *Annual Report*, 1909, p. 18.

28. WLM, *Annual Report*, 1895, p. 64.

29. WLM, *Annual Report*, 1888, p. 62.

30. WLM, *Annual Report*, 1895, p. 105.

31. WLM, *Annual Report*, 1895, p. 11.

32. WLM, *Annual Report*, 1898, p. 20.

33. WLM, *Annual Report*, 1898, p. 51.

34. Pethick-Lawrence, *My Part in a Changing World*, p. 72.

35. M. Vicinus, *Independent Women*, London 1985, p. 61.

5. *The Social Work of the Mission before 1914*

1. Hugh Price Hughes, *Social Christianity: Sermons*, London 1890, p. 26.
2. Ibid., p. 55.
3. *Advance*, May 1902, p. 42.
4. J. E. Rattenbury, *Six Sermons on Social Subjects*, London 1908, p. 116.
5. J. Deane Hilton, *Marie Hilton: Her Life and Work, 1821–1896*, London 1897, pp. 176–82 and 243–4.
6. In WLM, *Annual Report*, 1895, p. 9, Mrs Hughes wrote of the crèche, 'which we inherited from the Hon. Maud Stanley and others'.
7. WLM, *Annual Report*, 1893, p. 90.
8. WLM, *Annual Report*, 1892, p. 87.
9. Ibid., p. 97.
10. WLM, *Annual Report*, 1901, p. 25.
11. *Advance*, March 1914, pp. 62–5.
12. Sister Hope, interviewed by the editor of *Advance*, March 1914, pp. 62–5.
13. WLM, *Annual Report*, 1894, p. 102.
14. WLM, *Annual Report*, 1896, p. 55. Sherwell wrote at greater length on his findings in *Life in West London*, second edition (revised) 1897.
15. WLM, *Annual Report*, 1890, pp. 5–6.
16. WLM, *Annual Report*, 1896, p. 55. C. Copeland-Smith, 'The Men's Social Department', in *WLM: The Story of our Work*, 1907, pp. 17–20.
17. Grace Goldin, 'A Protohospice at the Turn of the Century: St. Luke's House, London, from 1893–1921', *Journal of the History of Medicine and Allied Science*, Vol. xxxvi, No. 4, October 1981, pp. 393–4.
18. WLM, *Annual Report*, 1889, p. 39.
19. WLM, *Annual Report*, 1888, p. 50.
20. WLM, *Annual Report*, 1892, p. 70; 1895, p. 69; 1896, p. 93; Statement of Income and Expenditure, 1898.
21. *Minority Report of the Poor Law Commission*, Parliamentary Papers, 1909, Vol. xxxvii, p. 200.
22. WLM, *Annual Report*, 1894, p. 87.
23. WLM, *Annual Report*, 1890, p. 82.
24. WLM, *Annual Report*, 1894, p. 96.
25. Goldin, *Protohospice*, p. 400.
26. Ibid., p. 393.
27. Arthur and Ensor Walters, *Sir John Bamford-Slack: Preacher and Politician*, London 1910, p. 77; *Advance*, March 1909, pp. 54–6; WLM, *Annual Report*, 1900, pp. 12–13; *Who Was Who 1897–1915*, p. 36.
28. Peter d'A. Jones, *The Christian Socialist Revival 1877–1914*, London 1968, p. 407.
29. *Advance*, October 1889, p. 13.
30. WLM, *Annual Report*, 1889, p. 7.
31. C. Ensor Walters, 'Our Work in the Cleveland District', *WLM: The Story of our Work*, 1901, pp. 15–16.
32. *Advance*, January 1902, p. 7.

6. *The Open Air Witness*

1. T. Fuller, *The Church History of Britain*, Vol. 1, Oxford 1945, p. 141.
2. H. Latimer, *Sermons*, London, Everyman Edition 1906, p. 59.

3. J. Wesley, *Journal*, Vol. 1, Everyman Edition 1906, p. 222.
4. Ibid., Vol. 2, p. 353.
5. WLM, *Annual Report*, 1888, p. 37.
6. *Advance*, May 1908, p. 84.
7. *Advance*, May 1905, p. 22.
8. R. Mudie-Smith (ed.), *The Religious Life of London*, London 1904, chapter on 'The Methods and Lessons of the Census' written by the editor.
9. *Advance*, May 1905, p. 22.
10. *Advance*, March 1915, pp. 5–6.
11. Donald Soper, *The Advocacy of the Gospel*, London 1961, pp. 73–7.
12. *WLM: The Story of our Work*, 1907, pp. 32–4.
13. Ibid., and *Advance*, November 1908, p. 104.
14. *Advance*, February 1916, p. 11.
15. *Advance*, February 1917, p. 7.
16. *Advance*, February 1918, p. 8.
17. *Advance*, September 1917, pp. 1, 2, 12.
18. William Purcell, *Odd Man Out*, London 1983, p. 21.
19. Douglas Thompson, *Donald Soper*, Nutfield, Surrey, 1971, p. 36.
20. Donald Soper, *The Advocacy of the Gospel*, London 1961, p. 74.
21. Thompson, *Donald Soper*, p. 35.
22. Soper, *Advocacy*, p. 72.
23. Ibid., p. 70.
24. A Bottoms, '60 Years on Tower Hill', *Methodist Recorder*, 27 February 1986.
25. *Tribune*, 16 March 1971; author's conversation with Lord Soper, 14 March 1986.
26. *British Weekly*, 19 March 1942. Letter dated April 1943 signed by 'Donald O. Soper' and sent to members and supporters. This states: 'Since the last issue of this Chronicle (i.e. April 1942) "Hyde Park" on Sunday afternoons has been added to "Tower Hill" on Wednesdays as one of our main "Preaching Places".'
27. *British Weekly*, 2 January 1941.

7. Years of Turmoil

1. D. P. Hughes, *The Life of Hugh Price Hughes*, London 1905, pp. 659–64; *Methodist Recorder*, 20 and 27 November 1902.
2. H. P. Hughes, *Social Christianity*, London 1890, p. 19.
3. M. Edwards, *Methodism and England*, London 1943, p. 147.
4. D. P. Hughes, *Hugh Price Hughes*, p. 551.
5. *Methodist Times*, 19 March 1885.
6. *Methodist Recorder*, 20 December 1938.
7. *Advance*, February and May 1902, pp. 15–18 and 42–5.
8. *WLM: The Story of our Work*, 1901, p. 18.
9. The information in this paragraph was obtained from the Executive Committee Minutes of various dates from 29 April 1904 to 3 February 1905, Greater London Record Office (GLRO) N/M/2/7.
10. *WLM: The Story of our Work*, 1905, pp. 5–6; EC Minutes, 16 February 1905, GLRO N/M/2/7.
11. EC Minutes, 9 June 1905; 21 September 1906, GLRO N/M/2/7.
12. EC Minutes, 4 January 1907, GLRO N/M/2/7.
13. *Was Was Who 1961–70*, London 1971, p. 934.

14. I am grateful to Mary Hicks for recalling this incident.

15. J. E. Rattenbury, *Six Sermons on Social Subjects*, London 1908, p. 107.

16. Ibid., p. 49.

17. *Advance*, December 1910, p. 223.

18. EC Minutes, 2 and 9 October 1908, GLRO N/M/2/7.

19. *Advance*, February 1911, p. 23.

20. *Advance*, July 1910, p. 141.

21. *Methodist Recorder*, 24 October 1912.

22. *Advance*, September 1910, p. 172; October 1910, pp. 195–201; *Methodist Recorder*, 24 October 1912; EC Minutes, 6 September 1912 and 11 October 1912.

23. EC Minutes, 13 December 1912, GLRO N/M/2/10.

24. *Methodist Recorder*, 14 December 1911.

25. *Advance*, October 1911, p. 188.

26. *Methodist Recorder*, 24 October 1912.

27. *Advance*, October 1912, p. 175.

28. EC Minutes, 5 July 1912, GLRO N/M/2/10.

29. *Wireless World*, May 1982, p. 30.

30. *Methodist Recorder*, 14 December 1912.

31. Quarterly Meeting Minutes, 19 December 1902 and 24 June 1912, GLRO N/M/2/1 and 2.

32. *The West London Mission 1909–10*, pp. 35–6.

33. EC Minutes, 18 December 1911.

34. Crèche Committee Minutes, 2 February 1909 and 5 December 1916, GLRO N/M/8/29–30.

35. *Advance*, November 1912, p. 203.

36. Quarterly Meeting Minutes, 30 June 1914, GLRO N/M/2/2.

8. *The Mission in World War I*

1. GLRO N/M/2/10, 4 August 1914. *Advance*, September 1916, p. 2, reported: 'Unfortunately the war has made it impossible to let the Hall for any large number of evening meetings and concerts, and this has seriously reduced the income.'

2. GLRO N/M/2/10, 10 August 1914.

3. GLRO N/M/2/10, 9 October, 27 November and 11 December 1914; *Advance*, Vol. xii, No. 9, December 1914, p. 178.

4. A. Marwick, *The Deluge*, London 1967, p. 31.

5. J. Clifford, *Our Fight for Belgium and What it Means*, London 1918, p. 4.

6. *Common Cause*, 7 August 1914.

7. Clifford, *Our Fight*, p. 6.

8. Siegfried Sassoon, *Prelude: The Troops*.

9. *Advance*, September 1915, p. 3.

10. *Advance*, September 1916, p. 3.

11. *Advance*, August 1916, p. 4.

12. *Advance*, June 1915, p. 3.

13. *Advance*, July 1915, p. 6.

14. Executive Committee, 8 September 1916, GLRO N/M/2/10. *Advance*, December 1916, p. 5; February 1917, p. 1.

15. *Advance*, July 1915, p. 6; September 1915, p. 3.

16. I. O. Andrews and M. A. Hobbs, *Economic Effects of War on Women and Children in Great Britain*, London 1929, *passim*; Marwick, *Deluge*, p. 313.

17. E. S. Peel, *How We Lived Then*, London 1929, pp. 144–6.

18. *Advance*, December 1914, p. 188.
19. Executive Committee, 22 October 1915, GLRO N/M/2/10.
20. Marwick, *Deluge*, p. 34.
21. M. MacDonagh, *In London During the Great War*, London 1935, p. 200.
22. Crèche Committee, 19 October 1917, GLRO N/M/8/30.
23. Marwick, *Deluge*, p. 34.
24. *Report of the Committee on Women in Industry, 1919*, pp. 1919, Vol. xxxi.
25. A. J. P. Taylor, *English History 1914–1945*, Oxford 1965, p. 96.
26. M. Cosens, *Lloyd George's Munition Girls*, London 1916, passim.
27. *Report of the War Cabinet for 1918*, Cmd. 325 pp. 1919, Vol. xxx, p. 293.
28. *Advance*, November 1917, p. 11.
29. R. Strachey, *Our Freedom*, London 1936, p. 251.
30. M. Royden speaking on 6 July 1916, quoted in Marwick, *Deluge*, p. 120.
31. *Advance*, September 1915, p. 4; April 1915, p. 1.
32. *Advance*, June 1917.

9. Hinde Street

1. *Advance*, September 1917, p. 14.
2. WLM Executive Committee decisions, 23 March and 27 April 1917; 4 April 1924, GLRO N/M/2, 11 and 12.
3. *Advance*, September 1917, p. 1.
4. J. Telford, *Two West End Chapels*, London 1886, chapters I–IV.
5. Mary Ann Smith, *The Life of the Rev Mr Henry Moore*, London 1844, p. 82.
6. N. Curnock, *Hinde Street Chapel 1810–1910*, London 1910, pp. 17–20.
7. Smith, *Life of Henry Moore*, pp. 323–4.
8. Trustees Minute, 30 June 1809, Marylebone Public Library, Accession 594/30/106, p. 22.
9. Telford, *Two West End Chapels*, p. 108.
10. Ibid., p. 117.
11. Ibid., p. 122.
12. L. Elvin, *Bishop and Son, Organ Builders*, Lincoln 1984, p. 208; Telford, op. cit., pp. 131–2.
13. Telford, op. cit., p. 184.
14. N. Curnock, *Hinde Street Chapel 1810–1910*, p. 31, gives a complete list of the first trustees. There is an account of Joseph Butterworth in *The Dictionary of National Biography*, Vol. VIII, 1886, p. 98. See also R. Watson, *A Sermon on the Death of Joseph Butterworth*, London 1826.
15. *The Dictionary of National Biography*, Vol. XXIX, 1886, pp. 96–8.
16. Curnock, *Hinde Street Chapel*, p.88; *The Dictionary of National Biography*, Vol. LIII, 1898, pp. 157–60.
17. Anon, *Hinde Street Methodist Church London 1810–1960*, London 1960, p. 18; Curnock, *Hinde Street Chapel*, Appendix 1, p. 118.
18. F. W. Macdonald, *As a Tale that is Told*, London 1919, pp. 83–5, 253; A. W. Baldwin, *The Macdonald Sisters*, London 1960, passim.
19. Telford, *Two West End Chapels*, p. 174.
20. Sunday School Committee Minutes, Marylebone Public Library, Accession 594/20; Telford, *Two West End Chapels*, p. 241.
21. Telford, op. cit., p. 248.
22. Ibid., p. 262. For an account of the climbing boys see J. L. and B. Hammond, *Lord Shaftesbury*, London 1923, Chapter XV.

23. Cited in J. Hurt, *Education in Evolution*, London 1972.

24. Sunday School Committee Minutes, Marylebone Public Library, Accession 594/20.

25. Leaders' Meeting Minutes, Marylebone Public Library, Accession 594/121.

26. Folder, *Hinde Street Wesleyan Church and its Work*, 1891.

27. Quarterly Meeting Minutes, Marylebone Public Library, Accession 594/3.

28. Greater London Council, Historic Buildings Division, Typescript entitled 'Hinde Street Methodist Church and 19 Thayer Street, Westminster', 25 October 1978; Secretary's Minutes, Rebuilding Scheme, Marylebone Public Library Accession, 74.

29. *Marylebone Mercury*, 7 August 1886.

30. *The Methodist Recorder*, 12 May 1887.

31. Secretary's Minutes, Rebuilding Scheme, Marylebone Public Library Accession, 74; L. Elvin, *Bishop and Son, Organ Builders*, p. 209.

32. *The Methodist Recorder*, 22 and 29 September 6, 13 and 20 October 1887.

33. Minutes of Debt Liquidation Committee, Marylebone Public Library Accession, 75.

34. R. Mudie-Smith, *The Religious Life of London*, London 1904, pp. 280–93.

35. Sunday School Committee Minutes 1887–1907, Marylebone Public Library Accession 594/22.

36. Hinde Street Band of Hope Committee Minutes, Marylebone Public Library Accession 594/146.

37. H. Bisseker, 'Hinde Street Church', *Advance*, May 1918, pp. 6–8.

38. Two-page typescript included in the West London Mission Quarterly Meeting minutes, GLC Record Office, N/M/2/2.

10. *The Inter-War Years*

1. D. Fraser, *The Evolution of the British Welfare State*, London 1973, p. 164.

2. C. L. Mowat, *Britain Between the Wars*, London 1955, p. 204.

3. H. Llewellyn-Smith, *The New Survey of London Life and Labour*, Vol. I, *Forty Years of Change*, London 1939, p. 21.

4. G. Weightman and S. Humphries, *The Making of Modern London 1914–1939*, London 1984, p. 159.

5. Llewellyn-Smith, *New Survey*, Vol. I, pp. 385, 389.

6. M. Thomson, *David Lloyd George*, London 1948, pp. 240–1.

7. Mowat, *Britain Between the Wars*, p. 250.

8. N. Branson and M. Heinemann, *Britain in the Nineteen Thirties*, London 1971, p. 275.

9. *Statistical Abstract of the UK*, 1930, pp. 88–9, 354.

10. R. Graves and A. Hodge, *The Long Week-end. A Social History of Britain 1918–1939*, London 1940, pp. 171–3.

11. Mowat, *Britain Between the Wars*, pp. 43–4, 164–5 and 176; I. Martin, *From Workhouse to Welfare: The Development of the Welfare State*, London 1971, p. 26.

12. G. B. Shaw, 'The Doctor's Dilemma', in *Prefaces*, London 1938, p. 224.

13. Branson and Heinemann, *Britain in the Nineteen Thirties*, p. 263.

14. Fraser, *Welfare State*, p. 155.

15. Branson and Heinemann, *Britain in the Nineteen Thirties*, p. 253.

16. WLM, *Social and Redemptive Work 1929–30*, p. 24.

17. A. M. Carr-Saunders and D. C. Jones, *A Survey of the Social Structure of England and Wales*, Oxford 1937, p. 43.

18. J. Stevenson, *Social Conditions in Britain between the Wars*, Harmondsworth 1977, p. 259.

19. WLM, *Social and Redemptive Work*, 1930, p. 17.

20. Weightman and Humphries, *Making of Modern London*, p. 50.

21. A. Marwick, *Women at War 1914–1918*, London 1977, p. 129.

22. WLM, *Rescue Report*, 1927, p. 8.

23. GLRO, WLM Executive Committee Minutes N/M/2/11, 18 January 1921.

24. WLM, *The Challenge of West London* (Annual Report 1935–6), p. 14.

25. WLM, *West London: its Glory and Tragedy* (Annual Report 1930–31), p. 14.

26. WLM, *Social and Redemptive Work among Women and Girls*, 1930, p. 11.

27. WLM, *Social and Redemptive Work among Women and Girls*, 1928, p. 8.

28. WLM, *The Challenge of West London*, p. 16.

29. Letter from Mrs W. Wintringham, 4 March 1986; WLM, *The Work of a Year told in Pictures 1928–30*, pp. 10–12.

30. *West London: its Glory and its Tragedy*, p. 20.

31. WLM, *Social and Redemptive Work 1935*, p. 12.

32. D. Thompson, *Donald Soper: a Biography*, Nutfield 1971, p. 59.

33. *Christian World*, 2 January 1930.

34. GLRO N/M/2/3, WLM Quarterly Meeting Minutes, various dates.

35. D. Soper, *Calling for Action: An Autobiographical Enquiry*, London 1984, p. 26.

36. Ibid., p. 76.

37. Thompson, *Soper*, p. 55.

38. Ibid., p. 58.

11. *The War Years 1939–45*

1. Letter from Mrs W. Wintringham, 4 March 1986; she was a staff nurse at the crèche from 1937–40.

2. W. Sansom, *Westminster at War*, London 1947, p. 19; C. Graves, *London Transport at War*, London 1974, p. 29.

3. V. Brittain, *England's Hour*, London 1941, p. 277.

4. B. Nixon, *Raiders Overhead*, London 1943, p. 15.

5. A. Calder, *The People's War*, London 1971, p. 182.

6. Brittain, *England's Hour*, p. 199.

7. Anon., *Hinde Street Methodist Church, London, 1810–1960*, London 1960, p. 14.

8. *Minutes of the Hinde Street Public Shelter Committee*, 1 July 1940–22 October 1945, Marylebone Public Library Archives Reference 249.

9. Anon., *Hinde Street Methodist Church*, p. 15.

10. Calder, *People's War*, p. 552.

11. *Kingsway Chronicle*, War Time Edition, Spring 1941.

12. Sansom, *London Transport*, pp. 43–5.

13. Typescript received from Mr W. Weston, a voluntary worker at Kingsway Hall at the time; M. D. Thompson, *Donald Soper: A Biography*, Nutfield 1971, p. 71; West London Mission Workers' Meeting Minutes, 6 July 1942, 15 and 20 November 1944.

14. WLM Workers' Meeting Minutes, 7 September and 7 December 1942. *The*

Times, 5 February 1943, carried a picture which was captioned 'Saving Vegetables', followed by the comment: 'Voluntary Workers of the West London Mission are sorting about two tons of surplus vegetables at Covent Garden every day. The vegetables are sent to hostels.'

15. Anon., *Hinde Street Methodist Church*, p. 14. GLRO WLM N/M/2/13, Executive Committee Minutes, 28 January 1942.

16. *Kingsway Chronicle*, Spring 1940.

17. WLM Workers' Meeting Minutes, 9 January 1941.

18. WLM Workers' Meeting Minutes, 17 August 1942.

19. WLM Workers' Meeting Minutes, 7 January and 21 February 1944.

20. WLM Workers' Meeting Minutes, 10 July 1944.

21. Sansom, *Westminster at War*, pp. 186–7.

22. WLM Workers' Meeting Minutes, 20 April 1942; 1 March, 13 September 1943; 3 January 1944.

23. WLM Local Preachers' Meeting Minutes, 7 September 1942.

24. *Methodist Recorder*, 11 May 1944 and 15 May 1941; *Kingsway Chronicle*, Spring 1941.

25. *Kingsway Chronicle*, Spring 1941.

26. *Kingsway Chronicle*, Spring 1941; *Methodist Recorder*, 15 May 1941.

27. Ibid.

28. *Kingsway Chronicle*, Spring 1944.

29. *Kingsway Chronicle*, Spring 1944; WLM Workers' Meeting Minutes, 5 September 1945.

30. *The Methodist Times*, 29 December 1887.

31. Sansom, *Westminster at War*, pp. 136–7.

32. WLM Workers' Meeting Minutes, 1 and 8 May 1944; 8 January and 21 November 1945; 20 February and 6 March 1946.

33. WLM Hungerford Club Council Minutes, 18 December 1946.

34. Cited in Thompson, *Donald Soper*, p. 58.

35. *Brighton Gazette*, 1 March 1941.

36. *East Cornwall Gazette*, 23 April 1941.

37. *Walsall Observer*, 7 November 1942.

38. R. Titmuss, *Problems of Social Policy*, London 1950, p. 508.

39. J. Harris, 'Some Aspects of Social Policy in Britain during the Second World War', in W. J. Mommsen (ed.), *The Emergence of the Welfare State in Britain and Germany, 1850–1950*, London 1981, pp. 208–61; P. Thane, *Foundations of the Welfare State*, London 1982, pp. 223–69.

40. Calder, *People's War*, p. 556.

41. Ibid.

42. A. G. Errey, *Experiment in Witness* (typescript, 54pp., kindly lent by Jane Hutton), p. 3.

12. The Post-War Years

1. A. Cairncross, *Years of Recovery*, London 1985, p. 366; P. Calvocoressi, *The British Experience 1945–75*, London 1978, p. 17, states that the winter of 1946–7 was the worst since 1880.

2. J. Harris, 'The Social Policy of the Attlee Government', in W. J. Mommsen (ed.), *The Emergence of the Welfare State in Britain and Germany*, London 1981, p. 299.

3. *Lloyds Bank Review*, 1957, No. 43, pp. 11 and 14.

4. A. H. Halsey, *Change in British Society*, Oxford 1978, p. 31.

5. Ibid., p. 30.

6. R. H. Tawney, *Equality*, London 1964, *passim*.

7. Cited in C. Davies, *Permissive Britain: Social Change in the Sixties and Seventies*, London 1975, p. 3.

8. WLM Staff Meeting Minutes, various dates.

9. WLM, ibid., 16 March and 9 April 1947.

10. Order of Christian Witness, *Newsletter*, Summer 1973, p. 11.

11. WLM Staff Meeting Minutes, 14 January 1948.

12. WLM Hungerford Club Council Minutes, 3 April 1946.

13. WLM Workers' Meeting Minutes, 20 February 1946.

14. WLM Hungerford Club Council, 18 December 1946, 22 July 1947; Hungerford Club House Committee, 11 October and 14 November 1950.

15. WLM Staff Meeting Minutes, 7 July 1948.

16. WLM Staff Meeting Minutes, 11 February 1948.

17. WLM Social and Rescue Work 1953.

18. Cited in A. Marwick, *British Society Since 1945*, Harmondsworth 1982, p. 149.

19. WLM Staff Meeting Minutes, 27 October 1948.

20. Office of Health Economics, *Alcohol: Reducing the Harm*, London 1981, p. 10; N. Kessel and H. Walton, *Alcoholism*, London 1965, *passim*; The Helping Hand Organization, *Female Alcoholism*, London 1975.

21. *Faith in the City*, The Report of the Archbishop of Canterbury's Commission on Urban Priority Areas, London 1985, p. 231.

22. Published as *The Advocacy of the Gospel*, London 1961.

23. 29 July 1965.

24. Christian Aid poster 1986.

25. For the account of developments at Hinde Street which follows I am much indebted to the Revd Arthur Shaw who sent me a tape recording, and to the Revd Arnold Cooper, who answered, in a substantial typescript, the questions I raised.

26. *The Guardian*, 20 January 1969.

27. This incident has been recalled by Bill Weston in an article in *Prospect*, the West London Mission's quarterly magazine, August 1986.

28. *Methodist Recorder*, 3 August 1978.

13. Conclusions

1. *The Methodist Times*, 19 March 1885.

2. J. E. Rattenbury, *Six Sermons on Social Subjects*, London 1908, pp. 73, 76, 77.

3. Supplementary Benefits Commission, *Annual Report*, 1978, para 1.4.

4. *Faith in the City*, The Report of the Archbishop of Canterbury's Commission on Urban Priority Areas, London 1985, p. 21.

5. Ibid., p. 23.

6. Ibid., p. 22.

7. *Advance*, May 1902, p. 45.

8. *Inland Revenue Statistics 1980*, Table 4.20.

9. C. Mayson, *Liberation and the Wine Skin Business*, London 1986, p. 7.

10. WLM, *Second Annual Report*, 1889, p. 5.

11. S. Fothergill and J. Vincent, *The State of the National*, London 1985, p. 16.

12. WLM Quarterly Meeting Minutes, 30 June 1914, GLRO N/M/2/2.

13. D. Sheppard, *Bias to the Poor*, London 1983, p. 219.
14. West Central Mission, *First Annual Report*, 1888, p. 2.
15. Sheppard, *Bias to the Poor*, p. 215.
16. *Faith in the City*, p. 24.
17. B. Pityana, *Index on Censorship*, London October 1983, p. 31.
18. Rattenbury, *Six Sermons*, p. 123.

Index